YOU HAVE A BRAIN

BEN CARSON, MD

WITH GREGG LEWIS
& DEBORAH SHAW LEWIS

ZONDERVAN®

Table of Contents

CHAPTER 1

The Amazing Brain

When you saw the title of this book, *You Have a Brain*, you probably thought: *Well, duh, of course, everybody has one!* Most people haven't given their brains much thought. I have. In more than thirty years as a brain surgeon, I have performed in the neighborhood of 15,000 surgical operations. Counting the scans I've studied, I've examined more than that. I had to know a great deal about the brain before I began my career as a neurosurgeon and I've learned much more since. My patients have been a most significant part of my education on the brain.

Christina was the oldest hemispherectomy patient I ever operated on. We'd had excellent results for years with young children, but I'd never considered the operation—the removal of half a brain—for a twenty-one-year-old. The younger the child, the more elastic and adaptable their brain and the easier it is for the remaining hemisphere to assume the responsibilities of the one that's been removed.

No one was sure how a twenty-one-year-old brain would respond.

But Christina had more than fifty violent seizures a day centered in one side of her brain—and that was under anti-seizure medication. Without the medication, she experienced even more seizures that wreaked havoc on her physically, mentally, and emotionally.

Her quality of life was poor, and the damage caused by the seizures was slowly, but surely, killing her.

So I told her and her family we'd give it a try. She did so well that within just a few months she went back to college. Where she'd struggled to do C- and D-quality work before, after the hemispherectomy, she made As and Bs. Her academic achievement had improved significantly. She finished college, became independent, and started working and making a living. Last I heard, she'd gotten married.

One of the joys of my life right now as I travel around the country is that so many of my former patients seek me out. Most of them are long past childhood now, in their twenties or even their thirties. "I have a family now," they say to me. "This is my wife; here is my son. I wanted them to meet you, and I want to say thank you."

Some of these encounters make me feel old, but aside from that I feel grateful that I get to see some of the fruits of my labor. To be reminded again and again of the brain's resiliency and the amazing potential in even once-damaged and diseased brains. A gift so remarkable, you can have a normal life with only half of one.

Just how amazing and remarkable is this human brain you have?

- Inside each human brain are approximately 86 billion neurons interconnected by more than 100 trillion synapses (estimated since no one has counted them all yet), which science has only barely begun to understand.

- Your brain started developing almost immediately after conception. During the first months of your mother's pregnancy, your body was creating neurons at the rate of about 400 million per day.

- Your brain generates electricity constantly, enough every waking minute to keep a low-wattage light bulb fully lit. So when you say, "That's a bright idea," your statement could be literally as well as figuratively true.

- Sensory signals move along an alpha motor neuron in your spinal cord at 268 miles per hour (mph). This is the fastest transmission of this type in the body. Skin sensory receptors, which travel at about 1 mph, are among the slowest in the body because they do not have a myelin sheath, which would insulate them and boost their speed.

- The brain of a normal twenty-year-old human possesses 100,000 miles of myelin-covered nerve fibers.

- Your brain can feel no pain because it has no pain receptors. The organ that controls the whole nervous system, and it can't feel pain! This is why we can operate on the brain without worrying about the pain level of the patient. It's also the reason we can perform surgery on people who are awake, as they feel absolutely nothing.

- Harvard University neuroscientist Jeff Lichtman, who is attempting to map the brain, has calculated that several million petabytes of data storage would be needed to index the entire human brain.[1]

When scientists try to quantify the capacity of the human brain, the numbers get so high that we can't get our minds around them. The potential of your mind is literally mindboggling.

My respect for the human brain has deepened over the years to an attitude I can only describe as awe. Every time I've opened a child's head and seen a brain, I marvel at the mystery. *This is what makes every one of us who we are. This is what holds*

---

1. David Russell Schilling. "Knowledge Doubling Every 12 Months, Soon to Be Every 12 Hours." Industry Tap. Apr. 13, 2013. http://www.industrytap.com/knowledge-doubling-every-12-months-soon-to-be-every-12-hours/3950.

all our memories, all our thoughts, and all our dreams. This is
what makes us different from each other in millions of ways.

Do you realize that no super computer on earth can come
close to the capacity of the average human brain? The most complex organ system in the entire universe is a tremendous gift
from God. There are hundreds more neural connections in our
brains than there are stars in the Milky Way galaxy.

I tell audiences of several thousand people that if I could bring
one person up on stage, have her look out at the crowd for one
second, then lead her away, then fifty years later I could perform
an operation to take off the cranial bone and put in some depth
electrodes, stimulate the appropriate area of her brain, and she
could not only remember where everyone was sitting but also
what they were wearing.

The brain sorts, organizes, and warehouses that deluge of
sensory data flooding in at millions of bytes per second. It's the
control and command center for all of our senses, all our other
organs, our body temperature, and the operation of every system
in the human body—respiratory, circulatory, and more. Much
more. Most of this work the brain does automatically without a
thought (literally) from us.

On top of all that, the brain enables us to imagine, to create,
and to solve problems. A human brain comes programmed with
the ability to extract information from the past, gather information from the present, integrate that data, and project it into the
future—which means we're the only creatures on earth with the
capacity to analyze, strategize, and prioritize so we can alter or
improve the world around us. This is unlike other animals who
only react to what's going on around them.

Yet, when I was a child, I did not think that my brain was
capable of doing much of anything. My classmates considered me
the class dummy, and I saw no reason to debate their conclusion.

My mother, however, always believed in me. She knew I had a brain, and she was convinced that brain could be my ticket to a bigger, better world beyond our tiny home and life on the big city streets of Detroit.

And she was right.

CHAPTER 2

Think Beyond the Can

I don't recall the first time my mother asked me, "Do you have a brain?" I heard it voiced or inferred so many times growing up that it's impossible to remember all the occasions, let alone arrange them chronologically.

However, one childhood incident always leaps to mind whenever I think about that all-too-familiar question from my youth. My brother, Curtis, and I had received a BB gun as a gift, and we were anxious to try it out.

After scrounging an empty tin can out of the kitchen trash, we headed outside for a little target practice. I took the can, and Curtis, since he was older by two years, carried our BB gun. In no time, we spotted the perfect set up. Instead of simply standing the can on a flat surface, we turned it upside-down over the wire prongs sticking up from the woven wire fence across the alleyway. That way the can might rattle and vibrate, or maybe even spin on impact, without sailing off the fence. We'd save ourselves the aggravation of chasing or picking up the target each time we hit it.

Curtis took the first turn. I don't have any idea how many shots he fired before the can finally pinged. I'd watched *The Lone Ranger* and *The Rifleman* on television and had good coordination and a steady hand. How hard could this be? I was certain I could do better than Curtis on my first round.

But I didn't. I don't recall (and never really want to) how many of my shots missed before I finally heard the first tinny ping of success. It was harder than it looked on TV — and downright impossible to adjust my aim when I couldn't always tell which way I'd missed. And it didn't help my concentration to have to tune out my brother's voice constantly offering advice.

Still our target practice became more fun and less frustrating as the frequency of our hits steadily improved—until we ran out of BBs and headed back into the house, discussing where we might collect enough change to purchase additional ammo. We still hadn't settled on a workable solution to our monetary shortage when a neighbor walked over to our house early that evening wanting to speak to "Miz Carson." He was carrying something long and flat. I couldn't tell exactly what it was—until he tipped it up to show my mother.

I'm not sure she realized right away exactly what he wanted her to see—or why. But I did. And if I'd had a magic wand at the time, I would have waved it and *poof!* Curtis and I could have disappeared. I realized our neighbor was holding a section of screen from his back porch. A screen with lots of little holes in it. BB-sized holes. Clearly, the screen had been in a direct line behind the fence and the tin can we'd been shooting at much of the afternoon.

From the look on the neighbor's face, he was not a happy man. Nevertheless, he politely inquired, "Miz Carson, would you, or perhaps your boys, be able to explain this?"

Curtis and I made eye contact. Mother hadn't been home earlier, so she knew nothing about our target practice. And we seriously doubted she'd had enough personal experience with BB guns to immediately recognize the damage for what it was. When she turned to us in search of an explanation, we had no choice but to confess. We were *not* going to lie to our mother. And we didn't want our neighbor to think she might have known anything about it.

We admitted full responsibility. Apologized profusely. Explained what we'd done with the tin can and exactly how it happened. We desperately hoped the neighbor and our mother believed we hadn't intentionally damaged his screen. In fact, we had no idea that we had until he'd shown up with the evidence.

Mother didn't say much. She looked more disappointed (and maybe a little embarrassed) than angry. The neighbor listened to our explanation and apology. He evidently believed our account of the incident because he accepted our apologies, but he wasn't about to shrug off the consequences of our behavior. "I'm gonna have to replace this whole section of screen," he told us. "And I can't do that for free."

Curtis and I told him we didn't have any money to pay for the damage. Looking back, I'm sure he already realized that, which might explain how quickly he proposed a solution. He'd buy the replacement screen. And once he knew how much it would cost him, Curtis and I could work off our debt by doing odd jobs around his house and yard until he thought we'd fulfilled our financial responsibility.

We agreed that sounded fair to us. We realized, though, that Mother didn't think it was entirely resolved.

No sooner had the man left than Mother turned, looked at us, and inquired, "Do you boys have a brain? You were shooting a gun toward someone's house! Did it not occur to you that you might miss the can sometimes? Did you not realize those BBs would have to go somewhere? Obviously, they went a lot farther than you intended for them to go. Or imagined they would go. They could have hurt someone! But boys, you are both smart. You need to use the brains God gave you and learn to think beyond the can!"

Then she looked right at Curtis for a few seconds before she shifted her gaze to my eyes. "Do you boys understand what I'm saying?" We both assured her we did.

We didn't feel quite so understanding when she ended the conversation by confiscating our BB gun and keeping it until we worked off our debt to the neighbor and showed her we could be more responsible.

· · ·

That certainly was not the last time our mother asked us, "Do you have a brain?"—any more than it was the first. My mother would pose it like an unannounced pop quiz on all-too-frequent occasions throughout those first eighteen years of my life. And I probably wouldn't have to think too hard to recall occasions she's asked that same question since then.

A majority of my friends today would not be surprised to hear me say that most of the time I was a pretty nice, laid-back, easy-going, basically-get-along kind of kid growing up. But I did have a temper—which got me into more than my share of trouble at school.

For example, I got into a scuffle one day with a boy who called me a name. Ordinarily, that wouldn't have bothered me. But this day, that particular name—long forgotten now—ticked me off. So I called him a name in return. He called me another name. One of us shoved the other. Someone yelled, "Fight!" And we went at it. We did a lot more pushing and grabbing than actual fisticuffs before a teacher pulled us apart. I suspect any scorekeepers in the crowd gathered around us probably judged it a disappointing draw.

Of course, we both got sent to the office anyway, and the school called our parents. My mother couldn't get there to check me out, so I stayed until the end of the school day and walked home as usual. When Mother got home from work later, I saw concern and disappointment all over her face.

She looked at me and said, "Let me get this straight. On the basis of somebody making a silly comment, calling you some name, you got into a fight that resulted in all this trouble at school?" I began to tell her how the other kid started it, but I hadn't finished my first sentence when she shut down my explanation by asking, "Bennie, do you have a brain?"

I knew the response she expected, but why did she bother asking? I raised my eyes to look at her and softly replied, "Yes, ma'am."

"Then you need to think, Bennie!"

She wasn't through yet. "And I don't care what that other boy said or called you. His words shouldn't matter at all. They won't matter to anyone else tomorrow. They only mattered to you today because you let them! What really matters is how you respond—your behavior! And you are the only one who can determine and control that—but only if you use your brain to look beyond the moment ..."

. . .

My mother had a lot of ways to say the same thing. But I was struggling to put into words my own frustration and indignation that it was ... *unfair how she always wants to shrug off others' role—even when they are clearly to blame—and focus on my response instead. Why can't she see?*

Mother was still talking, and as her words interrupted my internal argument, it seemed almost as if she was hearing my thoughts. "If you let others' actions and words determine what you do, there's no real point in having a mind of your own. Use that brain God gave you ..."

There it was; I knew that was coming.

"... to make your own decisions, to choose your own path. Don't let anything other people say or do rob you of that choice—that responsibility. Even in the heat of the moment you need to use that brain to think. Don't let anyone else push you into doing something foolish or wrong that you'll regret as soon as the moment is over. Or tomorrow. Maybe even forever."

In other words, think beyond the moment. Look beyond the can.

An awful lot of what Mother desperately wanted us to learn about life seemed to relate to that overarching theme of "You've got a brain—use it." She was big on taking responsibility. God had given us our brains. And with those brains came the ability to figure out which way the wind was blowing and maybe even how to harness it for our own benefit.

So Curtis and I didn't hear that familiar question only when we'd gotten into trouble. It was often mother's immediate (and sometimes only) response when one of us would run to her complaining about something the other had said or done. "Do you boys have a brain?"

Yes, of course. We didn't even have to answer out loud. We might nod or simply lower our chins.

"Then surely you have the intelligence to settle this between yourselves."

Or we'd be whining about a bike or something else that was in need of repair before we could use it. She'd just look at us and ask, "Do you have a brain?" (Pause for effect) "Then I bet you can figure out what needs to be done to fix it." Sometimes she wouldn't say a word, but just give us her "use your brain" look.

It got to the point that we didn't even bother to inform her about a lot of little things—like the fact that an essential piece of some game was lost. We'd just use our heads to figure out something we could use as a substitute.

Excuses were another trigger occasion for Mother's familiar question. "I just ran out of time to finish my math homework last night. By the time I got my chores done, it was bedtime and I was just too tired to stay up any longer." Such explanations launched many a brain lecture about all manner of wisdom regarding the importance of prioritizing, managing time, taking responsibility for our decisions, behavior, life, etc.

Whether life presented Curtis and me with irritating little problems and people or seemingly insurmountable obstacles,

Mother routinely challenged us with the same question. The implication was always that since we did have brains, we were expected to find a reasonable way to deal with any issue.

Somehow, despite her lack of formal education (she'd only finished the third grade), or maybe because of what she realized she'd missed, my mother had as deep an appreciation, respect, and belief in the potential of the human brain as anyone I've ever known. She hadn't taken a single course in biology, anatomy, or neurological science. (When I was growing up, she probably didn't even know there was a field of study called neurological science.) Yet she was convinced that the greatest resource she, her two sons, and everyone else had been born with was our brains.

The fact that we understood the assumptions and intent behind Mother's question didn't mean we liked hearing it. Curtis and I had heard the words so often that we sometimes dreaded the thought of plowing the same familiar ground one more time.

Yet we never heard the question and took the words as an insult to our intelligence. We knew Mother believed the answer to her question was a resounding "yes." She reminded us of that on a regular basis. We never took it as any sort of put-down or critical judgment of our mental capacities. More the opposite, in fact. Whenever I heard Mother ask if I had a brain, it reaffirmed her high expectations of me — because we both very well knew that she believed I had a better than average brain.

More than chastisement or reminder, the question served as a challenge for me. It instilled confidence and hope that if I would only make use of this resource I'd been given, I would be ready to deal with any hardship or challenge life threw at me. No matter what circumstances I faced, I had the opportunity to get out of bed every morning and think big.

Since my mother believed that, so did I — which turned out to be no little thing. Some of the challenges we would face together would turn out to be huge.

CHAPTER 3

Gone

When I was small I could hardly wait for my dad to come home from work in the afternoon. I'd sit on the porch of our house watching until I'd see him striding down the alley toward our house. Then I'd run and leap into his arms. He would swing me up into the air and carry me into the house, laughing and talking with me as we went. By the time I was school age, I knew my father was spending less and less time with us, but I thought we had a happy family.

I was only eight years old and my brother, Curtis, ten on the day our mother sat us down and told us, "Boys, your father has moved out of this house. He's not going to live with us anymore."

In tears, I pleaded with Mother to explain why he was moving out. I begged her to make Daddy come back. She said she couldn't and finally went so far as to tell me, "Your father has done some really bad things." I had no idea what that meant. So for a long time I prayed that my father would come back and say he was sorry so Mother would forgive him and we could all be a family again. When I told Mother what I was praying for, she told me it wasn't that simple. I still didn't understand.

Several years later I learned that my father had been living a double life since before I was born—complete with a second wife and another set of children. When Mother learned that shocking truth and informed him she couldn't and wouldn't live with a bigamist, he packed up all of his things, moved out, and went to live full-time with his other family.

When he left, our father took all of our family's money, including the small savings our mother had managed to store up by scrimping over the years. He soon quit paying child support, leaving Mother with nothing but a small house, no savings or income, and two active sons to raise on her own. To make matters worse, she had never held a paying job, had no job skills, and possessed only a third-grade education. The only skills she had were the ones required of a housewife and mother. So she began cleaning houses, taking care of other people's children, and sometimes cooking for two, three, or more well-to-do families at a time.

Many mornings she left before dawn and didn't return from her second or third job until after Curtis and I were in bed for the night, which meant sometimes two or three days might go by without us seeing her. She would call home to check on us after school, make sure we were home, find out how our day had gone, and ask for a progress report on our chores and homework before we could go out to play. And when she didn't have something ready in the refrigerator for us to heat up for supper, she would have the ingredients there for a simple and nutritious meal we could fix ourselves.

After having our mother at home with us for our entire lives, it was unsettling that she was suddenly gone so much. We knew the adjustment must be as hard for her as it was for us. We could see how hard she worked by how physically exhausted she always was. But she explained that she had to work as many hours as possible each day, for as many families as she could fit into her schedule, if there was any hope to pay the bills and keep our house.

As hard as she worked, Mother soon realized she was in a deep financial hole that she couldn't dig out of without help. Rather than fall behind on the monthly mortgage payments and lose our little house, Mother came up with an alternative plan. She rented out our home to another family for enough money to cover the mortgage each month. Then she accepted the invitation from her older sister and brother-in-law, Aunt Jean and Uncle

William Avery, to live with them in Boston until she could get back on her feet financially. Mother could find the same kind of work there, and without housing and utility expenses she could save up money over time, pay old bills, and build another small financial cushion. She hoped before long to be able to go back home to Detroit.

. . .

Aunt Jean and Uncle William Avery's own kids were grown, so they had a lot of love to shower on Curtis and me. The tenement "house" they lived in wasn't a house at all, but rather a rundown apartment building. And our new neighborhood was a lot rougher than where we had lived in Detroit.

Huge rats roamed in packs through the weeds out back. Once, someone killed a large snake in the basement of our building. After we heard that, we decided that wasn't the best place to play. On our way to and from school or the grocery store, Curtis and I frequently walked past, or even stepped over, homeless drunks asleep on nearby sidewalks. And all hours of the day and night, police cars raced by with sirens blasting and lights flashing.

Curtis and I thought one great benefit of moving to Boston was the opportunity to develop something of a big brother-type relationship with two of our Avery cousins. We didn't spend a lot of time with them because they lived on their own and only came home for holidays and special family occasions. Once in a while they would bring home some of their friends, but they always made a point of talking and rough-housing with us whenever they were there. We'd never before had a chance to spend time around guys in their late teens and twenties—and having them treat us like friends and brothers was a great new experience for us.

Those times our cousins came home must have created mixed emotions for Aunt Jean and Uncle William. They always acted glad to have their grown children back in the house, but my aunt and uncle knew some of their sons' friends were mixed up with gangs. They worried that their boys were quickly getting involved in the local drug culture.

I didn't know anything about that until the day we learned one of their sons, someone I'd come to love and look up to, had been killed in a street shooting not far from where we were living. I was devastated.

The adults didn't talk about it much around Curtis and me. But Mother made certain we knew the murder wouldn't have happened if our cousin hadn't gotten involved with the wrong crowd where the combination of alcohol, drugs, and violence predictably resulted in an all-too-common and deadly end.

Mother made it clear that our cousin's death had been an unnecessary tragedy and a terrible waste—the direct result of bad choices he'd made. Witnessing the wrenching grief of our aunt and uncle drove the lesson home. And I vowed never to forget it. I determined I would use my brain to think about the consequences of my actions, to make better decisions, and never to cause that much pain and anguish for my mother or anyone else I loved.

Fortunately, a dream for my future had entered my life—born one Saturday morning during church. I naively believed that this plan would help keep me from ever being tempted to get into that kind of nightmarish trouble as I grew up. Our head minister related an exciting true story about a missionary doctor and his wife being chased by robbers. When the fleeing couple came to the edge of a cliff, there seemed to be no place to go—until they spotted a cleft, or crack, in the rock just big enough for the two of them to crawl into. So by the time the bandits approached the precipice, the doctor and his wife seemed to have vanished. The frustrated robbers stomped around, but eventually left, and the missionaries were safe. God had protected them.

I was still replaying that story in my mind when the preacher concluded his sermon and asked if anyone in the congregation wanted to give his or her life to Jesus. Without hesitation I stood and walked to the altar at the front of the church where the minister was standing. He prayed with me as I asked Jesus into my heart. I was eight years old, so I didn't understand a lot about what my prayer meant. But after that day I knew two things: I wanted Jesus to watch over my life as he had watched over that missionary couple. And I knew that I wanted to be a missionary doctor when I grew up.

As we walked home from church, I told my mother about my decisions. When she heard the part about wanting to be a missionary doctor, she stopped in the middle of the sidewalk, turned, and looked right at me. "Bennie," she said, "if you ask the Lord for something and believe he will do it, it will happen."

I will never forget that moment. Indeed, I've recalled my mother's reaction countless times over the course of my life, often when I needed encouragement. She had clearly heard my heart and had understood and affirmed the dream I believed God had given me.

One of Mother's own dreams (which Curtis and I shared) came true when her personal financial recovery plan finally came to fruition. It took two years in Boston, but at the end of my fourth-grade year, she had saved enough money to move back to Detroit.

Mother wasn't sure about covering all the moving costs and also taking on mortgage payments right away. So she decided she'd continue to rent out our own house and she'd rent a smaller place not far from our old neighborhood until she could be certain about her budget. It felt like a big step back to normalcy just to be near friends in Detroit again.

. . .

Unfortunately, our return to Detroit brought a problem none of us had anticipated. For our two years in Boston, my third- and fourth-grade years and Curtis' fifth and sixth, he and I had attended a small, church-sponsored school where we'd been among the better students. But when we returned to Detroit schools, we found ourselves way behind our classmates.

I was so far behind in every single one of my subjects that some of my classmates called me "dummy" out on the playground. I didn't like that at all, but I was painfully aware of how far behind I was and how much I didn't understand in class. So I figured I deserved it.

Laughing and shrugging off the name calling probably egged them on. So it wasn't long until they dubbed me "the dumbest kid in fifth grade." By that time I had plenty of poor test grades to make me believe that. So it seemed pointless to take offense or disagree with them on that either.

Then one day I heard someone laughingly say, "Hey, Carson's the dumbest kid in the world!" I thought, *Wait just a minute. I bet somewhere in the world there has to be someone dumber than me!*

Unfortunately, that very afternoon, the teacher gave us all a math quiz. When we finished answering all the questions, we were to exchange papers with a neighbor and grade each other's quizzes as the teacher read the answers. Then the graders would count the correct answers, write the number at the top of the page, and hand them back. At that point the teacher would go through her grade book and we were to tell her our scores when she called our names.

Just that morning I'd been arguing my case—that I *was not* the dumbest fifth-grade kid in the world. But when I got my paper back, it had a great big ZERO at the top. I hadn't gotten a single answer right on my quiz. Those guys I'd been debating with were going to laugh like never before when they heard that. *Maybe if I mumble my score when she calls my name, everyone will misunderstand.* That was the best plan I could come up with on the spur of the moment. So when I heard my name called, I lowered my voice and softly mumbled "N-n-u-n-n!"

It worked! The teacher exclaimed, "Nine! That's wonderful, Bennie. That's real improvement! (There had been thirty questions on the test, so nine right still would have been an F. But it would have been higher than usual.) She continued: "Just keep on working those practice problems, Bennie, you're obviously catching on ..."

At that point the girl who had graded my quiz was waving her hand furiously. When the teacher finally quit praising me and called on her, she announced in an exasperated tone, "Bennie said, 'NONE!' Not nine! He didn't get any right!"

The entire class exploded in such riotous laughter that I know the teacher was embarrassed for me. I felt so humiliated, I would have gladly disappeared into the cracks in the floorboards, never to return to that classroom or see any of those classmates again.

The all-time low came a few weeks later when Curtis and I received our midterm grade reports. We came home from school and left the report cards on the kitchen table without a word to our mother. Maybe we were hoping she'd mistake them for trash, accidentally pitch them in the garbage, and lose them forever.

She didn't.

No sooner had she come in the house that evening than she picked up those report cards and studied them silently for a few minutes. She then called for us. When we walked into the kitchen, she reached out and pulled us both close and looked right in our eyes.

I had figured she would be upset. But the look in her eyes and the sound of her voice was more like sadness than anger as she told us, "Boys, if you keep making grades like this, you'll spend the rest of your lives sweeping floors in a factory. And that's not what God wants for you. He gave you amazing brains, and he wants you to use them."

I tried to brush off her concern by reminding her that these were just midterm grades. They didn't really matter. She would have none of that. She insisted the grades did matter because they told us what our final grade for the term would be if we didn't change. And she obviously thought things needed to change. And fast.

"I don't know what to do," she admitted. "But God promises in the Bible to give wisdom to those who ask. So tonight I'm going to pray for wisdom. I'm going to ask the Lord what I need to do to help you."

With that, she sent us to our room for the night and said she'd tell us tomorrow what God said needed to happen.

Curtis and I went to bed right away. But I had a hard time falling asleep while worrying what in the world God might say to our mother.

CHAPTER 4

How We Got Smart

We didn't know what to think the next day when Mother sat Curtis and me down and began to say, "You remember when I told you I was going to pray and ask the Lord to give me wisdom about what to do about your grades?"

Like we could have ever forgotten that! We'd thought of little else since. "Yes, ma'am," we assured her. I'd been dying to hear what God had said, but now I wasn't so sure I wanted to know.

"I did pray," she said. "Well ... I believe God gave me the wisdom I needed."

She looked a little uncertain about how to put into words what she was going to say next. As if we probably wouldn't want to hear it. This couldn't be good ...

"The wisdom I believe God gave me was this," she told us. "We're going to start by turning off the television. And from now on, you may watch two or three shows each week." When we groaned, she quickly added, "You get to choose the shows, but three times per week is it. And you will use all that extra time you have for reading."

Oh man! I couldn't believe this. *That doesn't even sound reasonable, let alone wise!* I was about to voice my protest.

But Mother wasn't finished.

"You can also choose what you read. At least two books each week. Then I will expect you to write two book reports on the books you read and present those reports out loud to me." This was worse than I ever imagined.

I may have been in my fifth-grade year, but I had never read an entire book other than the books my teachers had assigned to read in class. I couldn't imagine finishing one book in a week's time, let alone two. I started to explain this reality to my mother before she got wedded to this crazy idea. But as far as she was concerned, she had prayed for wisdom and gotten her answer. She had made up her mind. The moment I realized that, I gave up the cause and simply shut my mouth.

I must have looked defeated, because my mother suddenly said in her gentlest, most lovingly tone, "Bennie, honey, don't you see? If you can read, you can learn just about anything you want to know. The doors of the world are open to people who can read."

I was eleven years old; I didn't care much about the "doors of the world." I was a lot more interested in being outdoors in the world. And there wouldn't be much chance for that if I was stuck inside reading and writing two book reports every week. And where were we going to get two books a week we would want to read? We couldn't afford to buy that many books.

Mother had a plan for that as well. The nearest branch of the Detroit Public Library was within walking distance of where we lived. She told us we could go there any day after school and bring home a stack of interesting books.

I still wasn't happy about the idea, but we turned off the TV, and the next day Curtis and I visited the library. At least Mother had said we could read any books we wanted. She wasn't going to choose for us.

On that first visit to our public library, I must have looked unhappy and lost, because a librarian walked up to me right away and offered to help. She led the way to the children's section and asked if I was looking for a particular book or certain author.

"Uh …" I hadn't known there was going to be a pop quiz, and I couldn't come up with an answer. When she realized I was stumped, the librarian asked, "What subjects are you most interested in? What would you like to learn more about?"

Finally, a question I could answer! Animals. I'd always loved and been fascinated by all kinds of living creatures. "Well ... uh ... do you have some books about animals?" I asked.

She smiled. "Lots of them." She led me right to a shelf filled entirely with books about all kinds of animals. I had so many to choose from that it took me a while to decide what to check out.

I surprised myself and actually read both books that first week. And I wrote the reports Mother had required and read them out loud to her—still hoping she'd relent and realize she'd been expecting too much. No such luck! She seemed so pleased by what we'd accomplished the first week that we had no chance of escaping week two.

I wrote two more book reports that next week as well. The same steady pace continued—two books and two reports, week after week. When we handed the reports to Mother, she would ask us to read our reports aloud to her. When we finished, we'd hand her the paper and she would spend a few moments looking over it. With intensity on her face, she'd nod and underline something here or there. Then she would smile, put a big check mark on the reports, and hand them back to us.

No matter the topic we chose, Mother clearly enjoyed discussing or asking about one of the main points we made. We didn't know until years later that she required us to read the reports out loud because she couldn't read them herself. Her third-grade education only enabled her to pick out a few words here and there.

What we did know even then was that our mother loved us, wanted only the best for us, and expected us to develop and use our God-given brains.

She told us over and over, "If you boys keep reading books, someday people will be watching you on television!" That sounded far-fetched to Curtis and me. But the longer her reading plan continued, the more convinced she seemed to be about the wisdom of it.

. . .

Mother constantly found new ways to underscore her "use your brain" theme and to convince us of our potential. For example, she began telling us about the lives and habits of the successful, wealthy people whose homes she cleaned every day. "They are no different from us," she insisted. "Anything they can do, you two boys can do. And if you truly want to, and you work hard, you can do it even better. You just have to use your brains."

On occasion Mother drove us out to the neighborhoods where she worked. We would gawk at the huge houses as she informed us, "I've noticed something interesting about the people I work for. The people who live in these houses don't watch much television. They all have a lot of books and always seem to be reading and learning. They also work hard—first to get a good education, and then they work even harder to become successful in their careers. And because they do all that, they can afford to drive nice cars, build these big houses, and live in this beautiful neighborhood."

"You need to think about that," she would say.

She would continue: "You boys are old enough and smart enough that you've probably noticed that in the neighborhood where we live many people sit around drinking a lot, spending hours every day watching television, and living month to month on government welfare checks. Most of them will never afford to live anywhere but old, rundown houses and apartment buildings in neighborhoods like ours. But now that you see and know the difference, you boys know you have a choice about how and where you will live your lives."

Sometimes other parents gave our mother a hard time about the demands and high expectations she placed on Curtis and me. But Mother would hold her ground and tell her "concerned friends," "My boys are going to be something when they grow up. And no matter what they decide to do, they're going to be the best in the world at it."

. . .

Soon, most of the librarians at our branch of the Detroit Public Library knew Curtis and me and often suggested books for us to read. Sometimes they would even set new books aside if they thought we might be interested in them. So it wasn't long before I'd read all the animal books I could find and began to broaden my interests to books about plants and then rocks.

Railroad tracks ran through the part of Detroit where we first lived after we returned from Boston. And all those miles of tracks rested on a graded bed of stone and gravel, consisting of all shapes, sizes, and colors of rock. So I would examine and collect an interesting assortment, carry them home in a box, and compare them to the pictures in the geology and rock books I'd checked out of the library. Before long I could name virtually every rock I'd pick up, list its distinctive characteristics, tell how it was formed, and sometimes even make an educated guess about where it came from.

Obviously, by the time I'd started a rock collection, I had to realize on some level that I was learning some new and interesting information from the books I was reading each week. But I don't think I began to understand how much I was learning or what impact that could make in my life until one memorable day.

Mr. Jaeck, my fifth-grade science teacher, walked into our classroom carrying a big, shiny black rock. He held it up and asked, "Can anyone tell me what this is?"

I immediately knew the rock was obsidian, but I had never raised my hand in class and wasn't inclined to do so now. I had been gradually improving in some of my subjects, but I was still considered the dummy in the class. No one at school knew about my new reading program.

So I just sat there looking at the rock in Mr. Jaeck's hand, waiting for the smart kids to respond to his question. None of them did. I waited long enough for the slow kids to offer an answer. None of them did either. I couldn't believe this. Was this my chance?

When I finally put up my hand, I heard someone across the room snicker. "Look, look, Carson's got his hand up. This is gonna be good!'"

Every head in the room turned; every eye looked right at me. Whispers began flowing around the room. The entire class clearly considered this a notable occasion that promised to be funny.

"Benjamin?" Mr. Jaeck was as surprised as my classmates. But once he called on me, and I answered, "That's obsidian," all the whispers died a sudden death.

I suspect all my classmates were shocked to hear anything come out of my mouth that sounded serious and halfway intelligent. But they were not sure if it was the right answer or a joke.

"That's right! It is obsidian," Mr. Jaeck exclaimed in delight. "What can anyone tell me about obsidian?"

I looked around, but no one else said anything, so I continued: "Obsidian is formed after a volcanic eruption. Lava flows down, and when it hits water, there is a super-cooling process. The elements coalesce, forcing out the air. And the surface glazes over."

"Right again, Benjamin!" Mr. Jaeck remarked. My classmates sat stunned, their mouths hanging open. Before he went on with his lesson, Mr. Jaeck asked me to stop by his room after school. When I did, he heard about my rock collection, asked me to bring it in, and offered to help me work on it.

Even at that time I felt fortunate (and thrilled) that Mr. Jaeck publicly invited me to talk with him about science after school. Most of my classmates really liked him as a teacher—partly because of his young age, somewhere in his twenties and only a few years out of college. I remember him as tall and slender with light brown hair and as a stylish dresser. On top of that, Mr. Jaeck drove a snazzy red convertible, which we all thought was very cool, especially for a teacher.

Someone like him taking enough interest to give me individual attention and encouragement was a first-in-my-life kind of thing for me. Saying that, I may need to give a little context here. The Civil Rights movement regularly made headline news throughout the 1960s. The push for integration continued to face significant resistance. So at that time, not just in the South, but also even in places like Detroit, many if not most people of other ethnic backgrounds pretty much assumed black kids weren't very bright. Even people who had no interracial animosity of their own sometimes bought into the expectations of that stereotype—in large part because they hadn't had enough personal interaction with African Americans to know any better.

It wasn't long before Mr. Jaeck made it clear he enjoyed the hours we spent together after school because he was convinced I had great potential in science. He was thrilled to find a student who seemed genuinely eager to learn and got as excited about science as he did. Virtually every day when the final bell sounded, I raced for the science room.

Mr. Jaeck collected and cared for a menagerie of living creatures in his classroom. I remember him showing me a tarantula he had just acquired accidentally in a bunch of bananas he'd bought. He demonstrated for me how they liked to hide in crevices like that. To this day I look carefully every time I pick up a bunch of bananas. I've never happened upon a tarantula of my own, yet I still think about the possibility, especially when I make a purchase at an outdoor fruit stand or in a foreign country.

Another interesting specimen in Mr. Jaeck's classroom was his Jack Dempsey fish—a Central American freshwater species named for an early twentieth-century professional boxer because of its fiercely aggressive nature and its prominent and pugnacious facial features. He explained to me that like a piranha, a Jack Dempsey is primarily a carnivore, so I needed to be especially careful not to put my fingers in the water whenever I fed it. Mr. Jaeck picked up a pencil by the point and stuck the other end into the aquarium. When that fish darted up and chomped off the entire eraser in a single bite, I immediately learned the lesson.

Other creatures that dwelt in various habitats around that science room included a squirrel, crayfish, a salamander, toads, and frogs. I was fascinated by the chance to study them up close. And I was thrilled when Mr. Jaeck gave me the responsibility to feed and help take care of them.

The role and responsibilities of a small-scale zookeeper weren't the only lessons I learned in Mr. Jaeck's science class after school. He taught me about patience when we monitored some brine shrimp eggs in salt water every afternoon. Some days later, I noticed a few tiny little things wiggling around in the water—a few eggs had hatched—and within a week to ten days hundreds of little shrimp swam around our little hatchery. Then we fed them and monitored their growth.

For me, the most captivating thing in that science room was Mr. Jaeck's microscope. I got to the point where I could not walk past a pond, a pool, or even a puddle of water without taking a sample of the water. I'd bring it to the science room, put a drop on a slide, and examine it under the microscope to see what was in the water. Learning about different microorganisms not only fascinated me, it also gave me knowledge almost nobody else I knew had. That went a long way toward turning around my self-image from believing that I was a dummy to understanding that I was actually smart. Mother was right; I had a brain. And it was a good one.

If it hadn't been for a young, caring teacher who enjoyed sharing his excitement and love for science with a former class dummy, I don't know how long it might have taken me to figure that out for myself. Mr. Jaeck became my first mentor (other than my mother), and I'm sure I wasn't the last student to look at him that way. (During the summer after sixth grade, he took a few of us students to our first professional sports event: a Detroit Tigers baseball game. And he paid our way.)

Decades later, when a national television network wanted to do a feature about my life, a camera crew followed me back to Detroit where I reconnected with Mr. Jaeck, who was fast approaching retirement and still teaching science in one of that city's elementary schools. There I was able to publicly recognize and thank him for the role he played in setting me on the road to a successful future.

CHAPTER 5

Bookworm

Not long after the obsidian incident, it dawned on me that I had known that answer in science class simply because I had been reading books on science-related topics. So I began to wonder, *What if I read books about all my subjects? Maybe I would know more than anyone in those classes as well—more than the kids who tease me and call me names! Maybe my dream of becoming a doctor isn't so crazy after all.*

Anytime I was in transit, either in the car or on the bus, I was reading. Every day after school, once I finished my homework, I pulled out a book to read. During school, the minute I finished an assignment, I start reading a book while my classmates finished up their work. I soon earned a new nickname from my classmates; the class dummy was now the "bookworm." I would be sociable and enjoy a game of baseball now and then, but reading became my passion and trumped everything else for me.

I think it did for Curtis as well. We always shared a room growing up. So we spent hundreds and hundreds of hours together, each sprawled across his own bed reading—while most other kids we knew were watching TV.

As time went on, Mother proved a bit more flexible about our television restrictions. We still had to abide by the viewing limit of two or three regular TV shows per week. But if we had finished studying and our other responsibilities, and a televised special was on that she thought would be educational, she'd make an exception. Or we might tune in and sit down to watch coverage of seasonal events such as the Macy's Thanksgiving Day Parade. But once we got into our books, Curtis and I both felt television was a waste of time.

Although reading two books a week sounded like cruel and unusual punishment when our mother had issued the sentence, we soon found her expectations weren't impossible. It didn't even seem like a chore. Some days I'd be devouring a book a day and getting started on the next one.

Mother could not have been more delighted with this development. She valued learning because she had not received a full education growing up. In carefully observing the affluent, professional families she worked for reading all the time, she became absolutely convinced that reading was the pathway to that kind of success. So once we had our noses in books all the time, she thought, *Now I know my boys are going to be successful, because they're reading.*

From those initial kids' books about animals, my love of animals soon prompted me to migrate toward books such as Jack London's *The Call of the Wild* and *White Fang.*—I also read history and biographies of significant national and world figures. The first autobiography I read was Booker T. Washington's account, *Up from Slavery.* He was born into slavery on a Virginia plantation just before the Civil War but went on to found the Tuskegee Institute, a school of higher learning for African Americans. He was recognized as the leading black educator in America at the end of the nineteenth century and the beginning of the twentieth. He even served as advisor to a number of presidents on racial and educational issues.

I also read a lot of Bible stories over and over—until I could have probably given you details of every story and character in the Bible. But knowledge and inspiration weren't the only benefit I gained from reading so much.

My mother had convinced me that reading would be the road to eventually escape poverty and establish a better life—but I found books could better my life in the here and now. Not just in terms of useful knowledge, but as an immediate escape from reality. As soon as I picked up a book, I was transported to an imaginary other world or to a different time. Suddenly I'd be gone—released from the mundane, limiting bonds of my own life and free to explore new experiences.

The richness of this reading strategy paid off faster and better than I could ever have imagined. My steady academic progress began halfway through my fifth-grade year and kept right on accelerating through sixth grade. By the time I entered Wilson Junior High School at the beginning of seventh grade, I had migrated from the bottom of the class to the top of my class in almost every subject.

The same students who had once looked down on me for being the dummy had become friends who respected me enough to come to me when they were struggling to ask, "Bennie, how do you do this problem?"

I would smile, nod wisely, and say, "Sit at my feet, youngster, while I instruct you." That was my attitude. After the hard time they had given me back in fifth grade, now that I was standing at the top of the heap, I enjoyed dishing a little of that attitude back down on them.

I felt I had to let everyone else in the world know just how much I had learned. I was ready to launch into a detailed lecture on any number of subjects on a moment's notice—in order to enlighten my less-informed peers. Years later, some of my cousins laughingly told me that whenever they would see me walking up to join in their activity, they would whisper, "Oh no! Here comes know-it-all Bennie. Let's go do something else!" At the time, I honestly believed I knew more than any of the other kids my age and that, of course, they should appreciate that. Because, after all, I was going to be a doctor.

I thought I was brilliant; actually, I was obnoxious.

My newly fortified self-image faced an unanticipated challenge halfway through my eighth-grade year, when we were finally able to move back into our own home on Deacon Street in Detroit. The move was a dream come true for us and the result of five-and-a-half years of my mother's planning, hard work, and determination.

The downside is that moving meant I had to change schools. I left my classmates at Wilson Junior High who had been with me since fifth grade and had witnessed my rapid climb from class dummy to honor roll student. Suddenly, I became the unknown "new kid" at Hunter Junior High School.

· · ·

At Hunter, my new classmates didn't seem to care or even notice who was smart. They only cared about who dressed smartly. And the "in" look at the time was Italian knit shirts, silk pants, alligator shoes, and stingy-brim hats.

You not only had to dress right, but you also had to play basketball and learn how to "cap" people. Capping meant you said something funny—but critical or insulting—to get the better of someone. Since my clothes were definitely not "in," I became an easy target for the other boys' capping.

"Know what the Indians did with General Custer's worn-out clothes?" one boy asked.

"Tell us!" another one exclaimed.

"Now our man Carson wears them!"

"Sure looks it," a third kid chimed in.

"Get close enough and you'll believe it, cuz they smell like they're a hundred years old," the first boy said to finish off the capping.

After several weeks of being the target of their jokes, I decided that the best way to survive capping was to become the best capper.

The next day, I was ready when it started. "Man, Carson,

that shirt you're wearing has been through World War I, World War II, World War III, and World War IV!"

"Yeah," I answered, "and your mama wore it!"

The students standing around all laughed—even the boy who had started the capping. He slapped me on the back and said, "Hey, that's okay!"

After a few days of me capping the cappers, the crowd began to direct their attention elsewhere. But even when I wasn't being picked on, I still didn't fit in at my new school.

We'd reached Mother's longtime financial goal of moving back into our own home, and I shared some of her pride in that. At the same time, I had never been so painfully aware of being poor. That economic status promised to prevent me from ever becoming truly respected, let alone an accepted part of the in-crowd at Hunter Junior High.

My mother provided for our family without going to the government for all sorts of welfare help. But other people wouldn't have known that, so I was embarrassed that we sometimes had to use food stamps to make ends meet. Every time I left the house with food stamps in my pocket, I worried that someone would see me use them. So if I ever spotted anyone I knew when I was in a grocery store, I'd wander up and down the aisles until the coast was clear. Then I'd hurry to the cash register and check out as quickly as possible.

Looking back now, I can see how this new awareness of the Carson family's poverty also impacted my plans for the future. From the age of eight until I turned fourteen, I'd clung to my dream of becoming a missionary doctor. Now faced with a serious aversion to poverty, I decided I would be better off as a psychiatrist.

I didn't know a single psychiatrist, but on television they all looked rich. They lived in fancy mansions, drove Jaguars, and worked in big, plush offices. And all psychiatrists had to do was talk to crazy people all day long.

I remained confident that I had what it would take to become a doctor of some kind one day. But I was all too aware that I would have to navigate the next big segment of that journey — Southwestern High School — with the same classmates I'd failed to connect with, let alone impress, at Hunter.

So I started ninth grade focusing as much on joining the in-crowd as I did on my academic performance. Although I didn't know it at the time, that meant my new goal would soon surpass and threaten my old one.

One of my problems was that I still needed to prove myself by reminding other people, again and again, how smart I was and how wrong those former detractors had been. It took a while for me to understand how my boasting was only evidence of my insecurities and a subconscious means of getting back at the kids who called me stupid back in fifth grade.

The boy who had been humiliated when he blew every answer on that fifth-grade pop quiz in math was more than a little proud to have totally reversed everything by the time he took algebra. On one midterm test, the algebra teacher added two extra-credit questions. When she passed back the graded exams, I noticed one of the smartest boys in the class had made a 91. At the end of the period, I walked over and asked, "Hey, what did you make on the test?"

He said, "I made 91."

I waited for him to ask me, "What did you get?" But he didn't.

So I volunteered, "I got 110 — everything right including the two bonus questions."

"That so?" he responded, as he turned and headed for the door.

"Well, maybe you'll do better next time," I called after him.

"Yeah," he answered without ever looking back.

"If you need any help, let me know!" He didn't acknowledge that he'd heard me.

Another time in ninth grade, I confronted one of my class-mates who never treated me well, no matter how hard I tried to be friendly. "Why are you so hostile?" I asked him. "Why do you hate me?"

"Because you're obnoxious," he replied. "You know so much and you make sure everybody knows it."

I don't remember what I said, or if I said anything at all. I may have just walked away. But I never forgot those words. Or how hard they hit me.

I thought, *In fifth grade, everyone laughed at me because I didn't know anything; now they hate me because I act as if I know everything.* My classmate's cutting words made me aware of how insensitive and overbearing I'd been.

Good grades and being smart didn't seem to earn popularity points among my high school classmates. So far they had felt more like a disadvantage. So I switched to Plan B. Instead of coming home from school and doing my homework, I started staying on the playground, shooting hoops, and hanging out with the other guys. Soon my grades slipped from As to Bs, then to Cs.

· · ·

Curtis and I had occasionally hung out with a pack of boys from around our neighborhood, playing pick-up games of baseball and basketball, enjoying typically macho boyhood sea-sonal adventures — snowball wars in winter and competitions, chases, and hunts before and after dark on long Michigan sum-mer evenings.

The only real mischief I remember us getting into was when some guys talked me into joining them in clandestine raids on neighbors' fruit trees during picking season. I didn't participate in that for long before I recognized the quiet inner voice of my conscience drowning out the louder call to adventure by simply whispering in my heart, *Those aren't your fruit trees and that's not your fruit.* After that, whenever anyone suggested such a raid, I'd look at my watch and say, "Oh, I should have headed home before now!" Or I'd simply vanish and head home even as the boys were making final plans.

The gang of guys I hung out with after school in ninth grade, trying to impress with my best moves on playground basketball courts and by blowing off my schoolwork, wasn't a real street gang, but it wasn't innocent.

As our half-court game wound down and dusk turned to darkness, one of the leaders of the group asked who was up for some more fun—a real adventure. I said, "Sure!" because everyone else did. But as the ringleader trotted off down the street with the rest of us jogging behind him, I wondered what I was getting myself into. A few minutes later, when we turned into an industrial park filled with rundown warehouses, I began to wish I hadn't come. We slipped into the shadows alongside one of the buildings and circled around to the back. Our leader slowed down to a walk as he approached a loading dock door.

Somehow he'd learned this door wasn't secure and all kinds of neat goods were inside. Nervous excitement began to drift through the group as he pushed on the door, which was chained and padlocked. Sure enough, the chain was so loose that a foot-wide gap appeared between the door and its frame. "What are we waiting for?" someone asked. Our leader wriggled sideways through the gap as the rest of the guys lined up to follow.

None of us knew what we were going to find in that warehouse, but I knew for certain whatever was inside was not ours for the taking. I also knew merely going inside, even just for the adventure of exploring, would be trespassing.

On top of the moral and legal implications, as I weighed the risks from a practical standpoint, I quickly realized: Nothing good is likely to come of this, and a lot of bad stuff could. This doesn't make sense. So as the guys in front of me jostled for position, I quickly stepped back into the shadows, eased my way back around the building to the street, and headed for home.

I never heard of any serious repercussions from the warehouse incident that night. But I decided to separate myself from that particular group of guys. Later, when I had any second thoughts, I remembered what happened to my cousin in Boston and I knew I'd used my brain to make the smart decision as well as the right one.

You'd probably think that one sobering experience would have cured me of wanting to fit in so badly. But I had more to learn before that lesson finally penetrated my brain. So I latched onto a different strategy.

CHAPTER 6

Taming My Temper

During the fall of my ninth-grade year, I continued to steer clear of the guys involved in the warehouse trespassing incident. I still wanted to fit in somewhere, so I focused my efforts on the part of the popular crowd more into fashion than into warehouses. Nothing immoral or illegal required.

A simple wardrobe makeover would do the trick. Which is why I brought up the subject with my mother day after day. I started out hinting, since my birthday was in September. Then I out and out asked. Finally, I resorted to begging my mother for new clothes.

She would tell me, "Just because someone dresses better than you do, doesn't make them better, Bennie." But that was another case where my mother's wisdom didn't seem wise to me.

One evening Mother walked in from work looking tired and carrying a shopping bag. "I know you need another pair of pants for school," she told me. "So I bought you these." She pulled out a pair and handed them to me.

I held them up, took one look, and announced, "I will NOT wear those! They're the wrong kind!"

"What do you mean, wrong kind?" Mother asked. "You need new pants. You can wear those."

"No!" I yelled as I flung the pants back at her.

My mother calmly folded the pants along the crease and carefully draped them over the back of a kitchen chair. "I can't take them back. They were on special."

"I don't care!" The volume and emotion in my voice brought Curtis rushing into the room. "I won't wear them! They're not what I want!"

"Bennie," my mother said quietly, "we don't always get what we want."

"I will!" I screamed, so enraged that I picked up a hammer off the counter, raised my right arm and stepped toward my mother. Curtis grabbed me from behind and wrestled me back across the kitchen. When he stepped between Mother and me, I looked past him to see the shock and distress on her face. That, plus the horrified alarm in my brother's eyes, froze me in my tracks. I dropped my hands and my voice, made a quick and subdued apology, and turned and hurried back to the bedroom.

Curtis stayed and talked to Mother for a while. I knew they were both upset and worried by the sudden intensity of my reaction. Truth be known, I was probably as shocked and upset as they were, not to mention ashamed. I almost struck my mother. I couldn't believe it.

I'd always considered myself to be laid back. I didn't think I got angry easily. But there had been a couple incidents when I had been so angry that I lost control. Once, a kid had thrown a pebble and hit me; I'd gotten so ticked off that I picked up a rock and threw it at him, breaking his glasses and bloodying his nose.

Another time I was getting books out of my locker at school when the kid next to me reached over and shut my locker before I was done with it. I wheeled on him in anger and swung my right fist at his face, forgetting I still had a padlock clenched in my hand. The boy required several stitches to his forehead. I got sent to the principal's office, my mother was called to school, and I ended up in a bunch of trouble. Both times I took my punishment, but convinced myself that my anger wasn't my fault — the other guys were the ones who had made me mad and they deserved what they got.

However, I did not think my mother deserved my retaliation. I convinced myself I'd never meant her any harm. No matter how frustrated I'd been by the clothing issue. *I'll have to watch myself*, I thought. *But that will never happen again.*

Before long, I approached my mother with a compromise plan. If nothing else, maybe she could buy me an Italian knit shirt. I saw the disappointment in her eyes when I asked. She told me she wanted me to be the kind of person who was too smart to fall for the latest fad. She thought I should use my head, and not just follow after other people who weren't using theirs.

Not long after that, my mother made a deal with me. She would bring home all the money she made the following week and turn it over to me. I could have charge of all our family finances — buy all the groceries, pay the bills, take care of all the necessities. Then whatever I had left over at the end of the week would be mine. I could spend it on Italian knit shirts or whatever else I wanted.

All right! I couldn't wait to get started. If I did a good enough job, maybe she'd be so impressed she'd give me permanent responsibility for managing the family money. What color shirt should I get the first week?

Well, it didn't take much time to run out of money — long before I bought groceries and paid the bills. I quickly concluded my mother must be some kind of financial genius to keep food on our table and any kind of clothes on my back. I realized I'd been whining and demanding she buy me a seventy-five dollar shirt when she brought home only one hundred dollars or so most weeks, working fifteen to eighteen hours a day, scrubbing other people's floors and cleaning other people's toilets.

I was so ashamed of myself that I determined never again to let my peers distort my values. I made education my top priority again. Instead of hanging out with friends after school, I headed home to study and soon my grades climbed back up to As.

Some of my classmates noticed my renewed commitment and laughed, calling me "nerd" and "Poindexter" (my favorite, named after the little, odd, but brilliant character on a popular cartoon series at the time). But I could usually shut up my teasers and tormentors with a simple challenge: "Let's see what I'm doing in twenty years, and then let's see what you're doing in twenty years."

I was using my brain again. And I had no doubt that was the way out. Mother's message finally sank in.

■ ■ ■

Back on the right path, life seemed to be looking up again for me. I had everything under control. Or so I thought. But the anger issue was still unaddressed. I needed to face it—and I did on one terrible day that nearly derailed my future and did, in fact, change my life forever.

My friend Bob and I were hanging out after school listening to his transistor radio when Bob nonchalantly turned the tuner to another station in the middle of a song.

"Hey!" I protested, and I flipped the dial back.

Bob glared at me and switched stations again.

I don't know why, or where it came from, but a storm of anger ambushed me and everything spun out of control. Without a single thought going through my mind, I pulled a camping knife out of my pocket, snapped the blade open, and lunged right at Bob's midsection. The point struck Bob's large metal belt buckle with such force that for one horrible moment I knew I'd mortally wounded him. But when he just stood there stunned, I looked for the wound. That's when I noticed my knife blade lying at his feet where it had fallen to the ground after it had broken on his belt buckle.

I looked at the remains of the knife still clutched in my hand, appalled by the thought of what almost happened. An inch or two either way and I would have sliced open Bob's belly. He could have been lying at my feet bleeding to death. I could have been arrested for assault with a deadly weapon—or murder. And I would have spent the rest of my teen years in juvenile detention.

I muttered, "I ... I ... I'm sorry ..." then dropped the knife handle and ran for home.

There alone, I locked myself in the bathroom and sank to the floor. *I tried to kill my friend!* I thought. I must be crazy. Only a crazy person would kill a friend.

Over and over again in my mind, I saw what had just happened: the knife ... the broken blade ... Bob's surprised and terror-stricken face. For hours I sat there, sweat dripping down my back, feeling physically sick to my stomach, miserable and disgusted with myself.

Over and over I kept thinking, *I need help! I don't know what to do! Something is wrong with me. I need help! I don't know what to do!* I don't know how long (or why) it took me to realize, *I need God's help!*

"Lord," I prayed, "you've got to help me. Please take this temper away! I will never achieve my dream of being a doctor if I continue to have such problems with my temper.

"Lord," I persisted, "You promise in the Bible that if I ask anything in faith, you will do it. And I believe that you can change me. You can get this anger out of my heart!"

I grabbed Mother's Bible and opened it right to the book of Proverbs. To my surprise I read verse after verse about anger and how angry people have nothing but trouble. One verse I read over and over was Proverbs 16:32: "He who is slow to anger is better than the mighty, and he who rules his spirit than he who takes a city" (RSV).

It was as if God was talking right to me. After I had read and prayed for a while, I stopped crying and my hands quit shaking. I was filled with a sense of peace.

I'd been in that bathroom for three hours. When I came out, I knew God had changed my heart.

Even though I had become a Christian and been baptized back when I was eight years old, this was the first time I realized I needed God's help. After that day in the bathroom, my faith became personal and deeper. I began reading the Bible and praying every day. From that day forward, I began to truly believe that with His power and presence and help in my life, and by using the greatest single resource He'd given me (like every other human being) at my creation, I could make wiser choices and turn to God to help me with my anger. Since I did indeed have a brain, if I would use it, I could do more to affect my life's potential, direction, and ultimate accomplishments than would my genetics, my environment, my financial status, or even the deepest, most crippling aspects of my emotional DNA. I never again had trouble with my temper.

■ ■ ■

Another life-changing experience during that same sophomore year reinforced the importance of this new insight. It started on an ordinary day with a scene that was all too typical at Detroit's Southwestern High School.

My early fascination with science, nurtured as it had been by Mr. Jaeck in elementary school, had greatly influenced my reading preferences since that time. I loved learning anything and everything about biology. And I liked and respected my tenth-grade biology teacher. Curtis had been his lab assistant two years earlier, so I'd met Mr. McCotter before I ever had him for a class.

However, standing maybe 5'9", a paunchy, middle-aged white man with thick, nerdy glasses and a receding hairline, Mr. McCotter was not ranked anywhere on anyone's "coolest teachers at Southwestern" list. His physical bearing was neither imposing nor impressive—and that may have been part of the problem in the biology lab that day.

We'd been studying a chapter on regeneration. The lab session that day would illustrate that process with an experiment using a species of small flatworms named planaria. Mr. McCotter was beginning to explain how we would work in partners at our lab tables "to cut each planaria into three or four segments …" when his instructions were interrupted with a chorus of "ick," "eeew," "gross," and groans around the room. When he continued to try to tell us that "all the pieces will remain alive and move around," the chorus rose to a crescendo.

When he raised his voice to say that "as a result of this asexual process, each segment you cut from the original worm will grow and regenerate," that was as much as he got explained before the commotion devolved into a chaos of snickers, loud talk, and head slapping. Mr. McCotter had no choice but to stop his explanation. "Stop that now and pay attention!"

The students he glared at directly would stop, but then someone on the other side of the room would slap somebody else's head. When the teacher turned his attention to them, another student hurled a wad of paper across the room … It just got crazy.

Mr. McCotter became so flustered and frustrated that he ordered the biggest troublemaker to stand in the hall. But that did little to settle things down.

We never conducted the experiment in class that day due to all the disciplinary issues. But the little I knew about what we were going to do with planaria intrigued me. Enough so that at the end of the school day I stopped by the biology lab to see Mr. McCotter. I asked him what was supposed to have happened with the experiment. He was so taken by the fact that I was interested that he got out a dissecting microscope and we ran the experiment right then. He acted thrilled, maybe even grateful, for the opportunity to carry out his planned lab, even with just one student. And I received a one-on-one lesson with detailed explanations and free rein to ask all my questions.

I came back every afternoon to watch the progress of the worms as they developed. One of those afternoons, Mr. McCotter asked if I'd like to be his lab assistant like Curtis had been. Of course! After that, I set up all the labs for the biology class. In the process, I learned basic laboratory techniques and procedures.

One of my first days in that role, Mr. McCotter and I set up an experiment showing how quickly and efficiently plants absorb the nutritional substances they need to grow. We placed a plant in water with radioactive material and left it overnight. The next day, we laid the plant on a piece of radiosensitive film paper and watched the exposure "develop" to see how far the radioactive material had gone through the corridors of the plant.

Not only was that the beginning of setting up labs for other students, but also conducting my own experiments. I later used that radioactive uptake experiment for a state fair science project. Mr. McCotter took such an interest in me that he soon began suggesting other experiments, and he would often stay after school to help me with them.

One afternoon he told me, "I've got to leave, but I want you to go ahead with your experiment." He paused before he added, "You are a trustworthy young man, Ben. Here …," and he handed me a set of keys to the biology lab. "Lock up when you're finished, and I'll see you tomorrow."

He let me keep that set of keys until I graduated—which turned out to open the door for another memorable experience the following year. A story I'll tell a little later.

Meanwhile, my encouraging experience with Mr. McCotter quickly led me to realize that, although I attended a poor inner-city school, I could take some initiative, use my brain, and still get a decent education. I just had to ask myself, *Why am I in school? Am I here just to watch all the turmoil? Or will I do what I can to change the situation?*

The answer to those questions seemed pretty obvious. Using the same strategy that worked so well in biology, I sought out my teachers in other classes—social studies, English, math— to ask them what else they'd planned to teach that day. They gladly gave me enough one-on-one attention and encouragement that I was able to acquire a solid educational foundation at Southwestern High.

Before the end of my sophomore year, Mr. McCotter introduced me to my chemistry teacher for the following year. He so persuasively recommended me to his colleague that I served as lab assistant for both chemistry and biology my junior year. Mr. McCotter also introduced me to the physics teacher at the end of that year, and as a senior I worked as the assistant in all three of Southwestern's science labs. Through it all, Mr. McCotter not only became an important mentor, but also my friend—as did a number of other high school faculty who were more than happy to share their time, their expertise, and their life wisdom with a student willing and wanting to use his brain enough to learn everything he could.

CHAPTER 7

Expanding My Options

T enth grade proved to be one of the most significant periods of my young life—a turn-around year in a number of ways. I refocused on my long-term goals and tried not to let the opinions and influence of my peers derail me. I had faced my anger issues, and I turned around the sinking grade point average of my freshman year and brought home honor roll marks by the end of sophomore year.

One other important development occurred that year that would help shape the remainder of my high school years. Even though I expanded my pool of friendships and started hanging around a different group of kids, I still hated always feeling like the dorky dude wearing unfashionable clothes.

My brother, Curtis, had been in ROTC since the beginning of his tenth-grade year, and as a senior had earned the rank of captain and served as company commander of our school. So I knew ROTC involved lots of work. But I figured if Curtis could do it, so could I. And the uniform would make it all worth it.

Which explains why, the first time I saw Colonel Sharper— the top-ranking Army Reserve Officers' Training Corps (ROTC) cadet officer of our school—as he strode with authority through the hallways of our school wearing a snazzy dress uniform bedecked with a three-diamond cluster on each epaulet, shoulder cords, and row after row of colorful ribbons signifying various awards and achievements, my instant reaction was, *Wow! What a great looking uniform! If I could earn the rank of colonel, I could wear an outfit like that, which would impress the girls and be the envy of all the guys at Southwestern High.*

As a second-semester sophomore, the private's uniform I

started out with provided a free pass from the "fashion police." And I soon discovered I also enjoyed pretty much everything else about ROTC—drill instruction, target practice, disassembling and assembling rifles, even the class work in military science and strategy.

The hardest thing at first was having to set the alarm for 5 a.m. in order to dress, eat breakfast, pack a lunch, catch the bus, and report at school for drills by 6:30 a.m. with my uniform pressed, shoes polished, and brass buttons shining. But at the end of my first semester in ROTC and going into eleventh grade, my performance was rewarded with a surprising promotion—not from private to private first class or even to corporal, but straight to sergeant first class.

A few weeks into my junior year, I moved up to master sergeant. By that point, our unit's ROTC instructor had offered me a challenge. He told me if I'd take charge of the second-period ROTC class—a notoriously disruptive, uncooperative, and exasperating bunch—and whip them into shape, he'd promote me to second lieutenant by the end of that fall semester.

I discovered the guys in that unruly class responded and paid attention to me when I appealed to their pride. I told them if they listened in class and worked hard enough, I believed they could become the top ROTC class in the school by the end of the semester. I drilled them hard and diligently worked with them on their firearm lessons. They shaped up and outscored the other classes that semester, and I received my promised promotion.

As a new lieutenant, I had the opportunity to take the Junior ROTC officer's field grade exam. It covered a lot of facts, but those facts were all in a book, and I always learned best by reading books. My top score earned me an interview with the area ROTC board and another promotion to the rank of lieutenant colonel.

The head of ROTC at our school, Sergeant Hunt, was thrilled

because my success reflected well on him. He was a dynamic young guy in his late twenties with career aspirations of his own. And he encouraged and challenged me to put even more into ROTC.

By the middle of the twelfth grade, I became the city executive officer over all the ROTC programs in the Detroit Public Schools system. That position allowed me the chance to meet four-star general William Westmoreland, who had commanded all American forces in Vietnam before being promoted to Army Chief of Staff at the Pentagon in Washington, D.C. I also represented the Junior ROTC at a dinner for Congressional Medal of Honor winners, marched at the front of Detroit's Memorial Day parade as head of an ROTC contingent, and was offered a full scholarship to West Point.

All in all, my ROTC training afforded me the opportunity to develop my brain in new ways, by enhancing my motivational, public relations, and leadership skills. These skills would all benefit my college application process. ROTC was only one of a multitude of high school activities, and Sergeant Hunt was merely the second of four significant faculty mentors I had during my years at Southwestern.

. . .

The first teacher at my high school to recognize my potential and challenge me to reach it was my ninth-grade English teacher, Miss Schoenberger. As a recent college graduate (or maybe because she wasn't that much older than I was), she warned me to be careful with whom I hung out. She didn't want my peers to be a major hindrance to my future success. Her belief in me boosted my self-esteem during the time when I struggled to find where, how, and with whom I might fit in at my new school.

Not only did I arrive in ninth grade with an unwelcome

reputation for nerdiness and self-consciousness about my family's financial status, but I also was a shrimp of a kid who worried if my skinny 5'1" physical stature might keep me under the radar of normal high school life. So being noticed by someone like Miss Schoenberger was an ego boost for me. All the guys liked her. Being a statuesque brunette, she was an attention-getter, as well as a stylish dresser and classically beautiful. Half her male students drooled over her. What's more, she drove a GTO convertible—the epitome of cool.

Naturally, I wanted to live up to her faith in me. But my desperate desire to fit in with the crowd, any crowd, had grown stronger as my freshman year dragged on. When my grades began to slip, I noticed concern and disappointment in her eyes when she handed back my papers. By the end of my freshman year and through much of my first semester as a sophomore, I avoided all personal contact with her. I wouldn't even meet her eyes if our paths crossed in the hallway.

After my tenth-grade turnaround, finding a better group of friends, and beginning my after-school lab sessions with Mr. McCotter, I sought out Miss Schoenberg (now Mrs. Miller after getting married) for additional instruction and interaction. Sometimes we'd talk about the reading assignments in tenth-grade literature. Or she'd recommend related books she thought I'd enjoy that would give me a broader perspective. She acted genuinely pleased by my renewed interest in my studies and my grades coming back up. I assured her I'd upgraded my group of friends, but on several occasions she offered me a ride home. I sensed that she did so in order to keep me away from any unsavory characters and situations I might otherwise encounter riding a city bus or walking the streets after school. I didn't mind her overprotectiveness; after all, who wouldn't want to ride home in that GTO convertible?

Perhaps the most lasting impact my favorite high school

English teacher made in my life happened when she told me to consider getting involved in forensic competition. She said it would develop invaluable communication skills for becoming a doctor or whatever else I might do in life.

I had no idea what forensics meant, but Mrs. Miller explained it was an extracurricular activity offered to high school students in the Detroit Public Schools system. The competition involved giving speeches or oral presentations such as dramatic readings or poetry or prose recitations. Students received coaching ahead of time and then competed against other students in the same category. A panel of adjudicators would score each presentation and give feedback.

It sounded like a lot of work, but Mrs. Miller was so adamant about its value that I agreed to check out the next competition for myself. I walked in with rather vague expectations and was immediately taken aback. The participants came from high schools all over Detroit, and many of these teenagers were able to express themselves better than most of the adults I knew. And I thought, *That's something I want to be able to do!*

I decided right then to sign up for forensics competition. Since I needed a teacher to recommend and sponsor me, Mrs. Miller happily did so. Then I received coaching from the educators who worked directly with the forensics program students one afternoon or evening every week. But Mrs. Miller advised me for the remainder of my high school years. She'd listen to and critique my presentations as well as suggest material I might consider using in the competitions.

I generally chose the prose category. For example, I learned and recited significant segments of Ralph Ellison's book *Invisible Man*, as well as some Shakespeare. My favorite part of forensics competition was extemporaneous speaking—where I'd be given a topic and thirty minutes to research and organize my thoughts. Then I had to give an informative or persuasive seven-minute speech on the subject. I used to practice at home by standing in front of a mirror, picking a topic out of the air, and then trying to talk on that subject coherently for ten minutes at a time.

I developed a sense of confidence and ease in front of an audience that has served me well as a public speaker ever since.

In addition to the forensics competitions, working in the high school science labs, and ROTC, I also played in Southwestern's marching and concert bands, and competed with my school's chess club. Most of my social life consisted of these extracurricular activities. Learning to juggle that schedule taught me how to prioritize and compartmentalize my life by forcing me to focus intently on the subject or activity at hand. Yet because I saw learning as the highest priority, I continued to spend every spare minute reading and gathering knowledge about any and every subject that interested me. I can honestly say I spent more time with my nose in books than anything else I did during high school.

• • •

The fall I started eleventh grade, Curtis enrolled at the University of Michigan in nearby Ann Arbor. So Mother and I were the only two left at home. Since she seldom got back to our house before late evening, most days I packed myself two lunches. When I finished up my responsibilities at school in the afternoon, if it wasn't too late, I'd get on a bus for the eight-mile trip downtown to Wayne State University. I'd go to the library to study and take a short break to consume my brown bag supper somewhere on campus before reading some more—until it was time to catch another bus back to our neighborhood sometime between 9 p.m. and 10 p.m. I always tried to be there when Mother got home from work so we could have a few minutes of conversation before bed. After a few hours of sleep, I'd roll out of bed the next morning at 5 a.m. to make ROTC before school and go through the routine all over again.

In addition to free access to a university library, Wayne State University gave me a foretaste of the college experience. The personal interaction and conversations I had with the older students on campus, plus the fact that I'd grown about a foot since my freshman year in high school, made me feel like I already fit right into the college scene. I believed I would have little trouble adjusting to life as a college student when my time came.

Another attraction of Wayne State University was its proximity to several of my other favorite places downtown: the Detroit Institute of Arts, the Museum of Contemporary Art Detroit, the Detroit Historical Museum, and the main branch of the Detroit Public Library. I probably spent the most time at the Institute of Art—motivated to do so by one of my favorite television shows, the *General Electric College Bowl*.

Every week I tuned in to watch teams of bright students representing colleges and universities around the United States competing against each other in a game show of academic excellence. Throughout my teenage years, I played along with the contestants and dreamed of competing on the program when I got to college. I could often answer the questions the College Bowl host would ask about history, science, literature, and mathematics. But two of the regular categories were subjects I knew little about—art and classical music.

So once I realized the Institute of Arts and the Contemporary Art Museum were just off the Wayne State campus, I decided to make up for that deficit in my education by regularly wandering through the art displays, familiarizing myself with famous artists along with their histories, distinctive styles, and most representative and famous works.

I soon came to appreciate and enjoy art—but not nearly as much as I learned to love classical music. I found I could check out a variety of classical music from the public or university libraries. Those recordings and the classical stations in Detroit provided background music for so many hours of reading and studying that I was soon able not only to recognize specific works and composers, but also even some of the conductors and orchestras performing the pieces.

My friends thought my musical tastes the most persuasive proof of my ultimate nerdiness. How else could they explain an African American kid walking Motor City sidewalks with his transistor radio playing Beethoven or Mozart at the very time in history when the Motown sound had taken the pop music world by storm? But I didn't care. I still dreamed of my knowledge of classical music and related trivia winning my school the grand championship on the *General Electric College Bowl*.

At the time, I could have never imagined the way my classical music knowledge would impact my life's direction and future as a neurosurgeon. (More on that later.)

■ ■ ■

One day late in eleventh grade, I was walking down a hall in the science building at Wayne State when I spotted a notice on a bulletin board advertising for a summer position as a college biology lab assistant. I was already doing that after school at my high school, but a university job had more appeal. *Hey*, I thought, *full-time pay sounds good, too!*

Although I figured it was a long shot, I walked into the office indicated on the notice, thinking the worst that could happen would be for someone to laugh and tell me, "Get out of here, kid!"

Instead of taking one look and running me off, the biology professor who'd posted the notice asked me into his office and proceeded to pose numerous questions about various basic lab techniques. He asked me what I knew about how autoclaves are used to sterilize instruments. He questioned me about ultrasounds and how they kill bacteria. My answers seemed to satisfy him. When I eventually told him I was a high school student at Southwestern High, he was surprised and impressed. After that, getting the job seemed like a slam dunk. By using my brain to take the risk of being embarrassed, I got paid to work as a full-time lab assistant in a college biology department before I even graduated from high school.

CHAPTER 8

The Smartest Choice

I played the clarinet when I first took band in elementary school because Curtis had played the clarinet. That meant Mother didn't have to purchase a second instrument. When my brother moved on to junior high and we could no longer share, I switched to the cornet and enjoyed that even more.

But the band director, Mr. Doakes, soon talked me into taking up the baritone. All it really took to persuade me was for him to simply say one day after practice, "Why don't you learn to play the baritone, Ben? I think you would do well with it." When I learned the school owned the instrument—so I wouldn't have to purchase or rent one—I figured why not? There was nothing to lose.

Mr. Doakes was a dynamic fireplug of a man—maybe 5'5"—and only the second African American male teacher I'd had (the first was in the parochial school back in Boston for third and fourth grade. A dark-skinned man with a light mustache, his muscled chest and arms gave him the look of a well-constructed weight lifter. However, the force of his personality, more than his physical stature, gave him his strong air of authority).

I never knew why he thought I should switch. But he was right; I took to the baritone immediately. I'd sometimes get frustrated when I couldn't play it as well as I had the cornet. But Mr. Doakes would smile and say, "You're going to get it! You are so close. Just keep working." His encouragement and my progress on the new instrument raised my self-confidence as much as it did my performance level. I thought he just might be the best band director in the world.

The band program at Southwestern was at best mediocre when Mr. Doakes took it over during my sophomore year. "I don't care what you were or have been in the past," he told us. "What you are going to be is the best high school marching band in Detroit! The best in the state of Michigan! Maybe even the best in the United States!" I can't explain it, just something about the way he said it made me believe we could be the best, if only we'd listen to him and work hard enough. He then proceeded to prod, push, and propel us toward perfection—which was where I learned some of the leadership skills I used in ROTC.

Mr. Doakes knew his stuff. He'd gotten his exceptional music education training at the University of Michigan, where he'd had a drive for excellence and precision drilled into him as a member of its incomparable marching band.

Not everyone liked and respected him as much as I did. One day when we'd gone over a piece of music again and again and again, one of my friends in the brass section muttered, "That man is a slave driver!" One of the trumpet players added, "Yeah, doesn't he know Lincoln freed the slaves?"

Another time after we'd practiced one marching routine for what seemed like forever, another band member spoke up to ask, "That time we did good enough, didn't we?"

Mr. Doakes spun around on his heel and glared right at his questioner. The culprit dropped his eyes and lowered his head so fast he reminded me of a turtle retreating into his shell. "Good enough isn't perfect!" Mr. Doakes announced to the entire band. "Do it again!"

He didn't have to push or cajole me as much as he did some of the others. Perhaps because I wanted so badly to please him, I took the slightest suggestion from him as if it were a command.

Mostly he encouraged me by letting me know he thought I had musical talent and he expected me to put in the effort my potential deserved. His expectation of excellence was something he demanded of himself as well—continuing to pursue his own academic education until he earned a Ph.D. and became Dr. Doakes.

· · ·

Whenever I had a free period during the day, I'd usually spend it in the band room practicing on my own and sometimes just shooting the breeze with Mr. Doakes. He always wanted to know how I was doing in my other classes, and we'd regularly talk about my involvement in ROTC. Despite being only in his late twenties, he often treated me more like a concerned and proud dad than he did a teacher. If he ever heard or even learned about someone giving me a hard time for being a "brain," "bookworm," or "Poindexter", he encouraged me to shrug off any pressure or ridicule from my peers. "Ignore it, Ben," he'd say. "You are going to go places those clowns can't even dream of."

Sometimes he'd talk to me about what to expect and what to look out for when I reached college. I thought my exposure to the college scene at Wayne State would make my adjustment smoother than most. I got the idea maybe he'd struggled a bit with that transition himself, and he wanted to spare me that. I saw his parent-like concern for what I knew it was—one more indication that he cared about me.

The most memorable and mentor-like thing Mr. Doakes ever did for me was to convince me not to pursue what would have been a great honor—for me and for him. In eleventh grade, he gathered the entire band together to tell us about the ultra-prestigious, summer-long Interlochen National Music Camp for gifted high school music students that was offered every year in

Interlochen, Michigan. Students would receive several weeks of intensive musical instruction under the leadership of nationally and internationally known directors and conductors, and some would even travel around the country to perform. Mr. Doakes went on to talk about how important this opportunity could be for young musicians, how Interlochen took only the best of the best, and how rigorous and invaluable the professional training would be. After explaining the rules of eligibility, he announced to the band that "four of our musicians here at Southwestern are eligible to try out for an Interlochen scholarship. Please give each of them a congratulatory round of applause as I call their names ..."

When I heard my name called, I was absolutely elated. After band ended that day, I hung around to ask Mr. Doakes lots of detailed questions about the application and try-out procedure, the scholarship, and the summer program. The more he told me, the more excited I became about applying and trying out for a spot. "And you think I'm good enough? That I could win?" I asked.

"Yes, Ben," he told me. "No question in my mind about that!"

I'd never felt more proud than I did a few weeks later, sitting in his office ready to celebrate with him over the news that I had indeed won an Interlochen scholarship.

For some reason, Mr. Doakes wasn't his usual upbeat and enthusiastic self. When I excitedly asked him something about the camp, he didn't answer right away. He looked at me, sighed, and gave a sad little smile as he shook his head. "Ben, I can't ... I just don't feel right about you doing this ..."

What is he saying?

"But you were the one who encouraged me to go for it. You told me you were confident I could win the scholarship!"

"I know what I said," he replied. "But Ben, I checked, so I know you're right near the top in every one of your classes. And you still want to be a doctor, right? That's your ultimate goal?"

"Absolutely! But what does that have—"

"Then this scholarship isn't right for you. I know you're going to be a great doctor, and I don't want you to get sidetracked. You will have to choose one or the other. And I don't think you should do this."

"I'm sure I could do both, Mr. Doakes," I insisted. "Let me at least try!"

"Ben," he said, "this Interlochen program will drain every bit of time and energy you have this summer. You've got only one more summer and one more year of high school. Your future will be in medicine or science of some kind, and your best chance to get into the best possible school to pursue your dream will require you to concentrate on that instead of on this music scholarship."

I know he could see the disappointment on my face. No way could I hide it. For what seemed like a long time, I just stood there—wanting desperately to say something that would change his mind. But I respected Mr. Doakes too much to argue.

By the time I walked out of the band room, I realized, *He knows more about this summer music camp than I do. And if he's right, there will come a point when I'll have to make a choice. Better I make it now with his input than struggle with the decision on my own later.*

Of course, I couldn't help rethinking the possibilities and considering, *What if . . . ?* But even in the midst of my disappointment, the one thing I knew for sure was that my band teacher knew me well and genuinely cared about me and my future.

What I was too young and naïve to realize at that time was how unselfish Mr. Doakes had been about this whole thing. Having one of his band members be the first Southwestern student ever to win an Interlochen scholarship would have been a huge feather in his professional cap. He had sacrificially placed my interests ahead of his own. Years later, when the truth of his unselfishness sank in, I respected him even more. Even today I remain grateful that my band director told me not to do what he and I both really wanted for me to do at the time and instead helped me make the wisest decision.

The first positive ramification of that decision came quickly when I landed that full-time summer job between my junior and senior years of high school as a biology lab assistant at Wayne State University—an opportunity I would have had to pass up if I'd gone to Interlochen.

...

A number of other memorable events that shaped my perspective on my academics and affected my future took place my junior year. To understand the first two, I need to give you a little background that ties them together.

Ever since that classmate called me out for being an obnoxious know-it-all back in ninth grade, I'd stopped being so obvious about comparing my grades with other students. But I was still caught up in achievement for achievement's sake. I still constantly felt the need to prove myself—if not to anyone else, at least to myself.

I remember getting a 99 on a chemistry test and learning that two other students in my class had made 100s. They never said anything to me, but I was certain they were secretly gloating.

I spent most of that day feeling like a failure—for making a 99 instead of a 100. I berated myself with self-defeating thoughts: *If I'd only studied a little harder, or taken a little more time thinking through my answers, I could have made 100.*

Not long after that, another incident occurred that did more than get my attention. It forced me to see and understand myself in a way I never had before.

One day the entire junior class took a field trip downtown to the Detroit Historical Museum. As you'd expect, there were a lot of impressive exhibits related to the automotive industry. On the museum's lower level, in front of a display portraying an 1890s fire station, I stood next to a classmate named Anthony Flowers. Looking at the primitive fire-fighting tools and technology available at that time, I whispered my thoughts to Anthony: "Wouldn't it have been great to live back there in those days and to know as much as I know now, because then I could be smarter than anybody else?"

Anthony turned and looked at me with a quizzical expression on his face. "But you're already smarter than everybody else, so why would you want to do that?" He wasn't intending to put me down, like the kid who had called me obnoxious. After that, while walking around the museum and on the bus ride back to school, his comment kept echoing in my mind. *If that's how my classmates look at me, I'm glad. So why am I concerned about showing off how much I know?*

Or as Anthony asked, "Why would I ever feel the need to go back in time?" Afterward I tried to honestly answer the question: Why did I always feel the need to prove my intelligence?

As I thought about that, I realized my attitudes and my behavior resulted from insecurity and a lack of confidence rooted years ago in the heart and mind of an embarrassed fifth-grade boy who pretended it didn't hurt when everyone called him dummy. Yet after all these years of knowing I wasn't really a dummy, I still had some deep need to prove that over and over to myself and everybody else. Now I could use my brain to analyze and understand the underlying cause. Surely that insight could help me control the emotional trigger that so negatively impacted the way other people looked at me.

I determined to work on that part of my mind. As I began to make progress, I observed that the ability to do so depended a lot on what was the central focus of my life. If my thoughts were centered on me and my insecurities, I tended to be relatively insensitive to others and the way they perceived me. When the center of my life became God and others, I became aware of what I said or did and how that affected other people. (That was what Jesus taught in Matthew 22:34–40 as the first and second most important commandments — love the Lord your God with all your heart, mind, soul, and strength and love your neighbor in the same way, and to the same degree, you love yourself.)

Gradually, my intention to do that began to make a difference in my relationships as a young man. (And it's something I still have to work on every day as an adult.)

. . .

Using my head instead of reacting to emotion, and thinking about others as well as myself, played a role on an important historical date that occurred in the spring of my eleventh grade year.

In the early evening hours of April 4, 1968, Dr. Martin Luther King, Jr. was assassinated on a motel balcony in Memphis, Tennessee. The shocking news reports triggered nationwide mourning. Violence and riots broke out in cities such as Chicago, Baltimore, and Washington, D.C. Everything seemed calm, if somber, at Southwestern High School the next morning. But as students began sharing their grief over the loss of Dr. King with one another, and emotional talk of the previous evening's tragedy spread through the school, the expressions and the intensity of sorrow rose in volume and turned to anger. A few students stormed out of classrooms into the hallways. Soon the noisy ruckus of breaking glass, running footsteps, and slamming locker doors echoing up and down the halls drew more students out into what was becoming an anger melee.

I was as upset as anyone about the tragic death of Dr. King, but I didn't want any part in the mindless violence of the swelling crowd I could hear screaming and surging through the front hallways of the school. The majority of those in the halls seemed to be caught in the flood surge of faculty and students. So going against the flow, I pushed and dodged my way toward the biology lab, at the rear of the school and out of the way of the riot — for the moment at least. But as I rounded the corner into that back hallway, I was surprised to find a cluster of a half dozen students huddled outside a locked classroom door. *What were they doing?*

Then it hit me as I registered the fear on several familiar faces. These were some of the few white students who attended Southwestern High. *Of course, they have reason to be more terrified than I am.*

I already had my key to the biology lab clenched in my hand. So I quickly unlocked the door and invited everyone from that hallway inside. Then I locked the door behind us and ushered my group of refugees across the lab and out into the attached conservatory where we crouched between rows of plants, out of sight from anyone looking through the window in the laboratory door. A couple of times we heard raised voices out in the hall, and someone unsuccessfully attempted to jimmy the lab door. But we stayed hunkered down, safe and sequestered, for what seemed like an eternity before the police finally cleared the hallways and escorted us all safely out of the school.

Some of those friends I'd hidden in the lab were so relieved that I felt a little embarrassed by their gratitude. I hadn't even stopped to weigh the decision or consider the possible consequences. But that evening, waiting for my mother to get home from work, I realized the main reason I'd not hesitated to do what I knew was right and hide my terrified fellow students was because of a principle my mother had taught me.

She believed God's purpose in creating and populating our planet with different races, ethnic groups, and nationalities was a simple test—to see how we as human beings would treat each other. She had always made it clear to Curtis and me that she believed what the Bible said in 1 John 4:21: "Anyone who loves God must also love their brother and sister."

So when I gave her my report on the day, my mother acted proud of me. And after admiring and knowing what Dr. King had preached, I kind of figured Dr. King would have been proud too.

CHAPTER 9

Off to College

I began my senior year determined to finish high school well and to do everything I could to enhance my chances for the best possible college education. After my Scholastic Aptitude Test (SAT) results and picture appeared in a Detroit daily newspaper announcing my scores as the highest of any graduate in the Detroit Public Schools system that year, some colleges offered me scholarships and many more invited or enticed me to apply with promises of significant financial aid. But I couldn't coast in any of my classes because I knew a final year of straight As would help bring up my Grade Point Average (GPA)—which had suffered severely the second semester of ninth grade and the first semester of tenth. I knew most schools factored both GPAs and SATs into their scholarship offers.

By graduation time I'd raised my GPA high enough to be ranked third in my senior class academically. That class standing, combined with my SATs, meant I could go almost anywhere I wanted for college.

I still had the scholarship offer from West Point as a result of my ROTC achievements. And the University of Michigan, where Curtis was already studying, pursued me aggressively. So I was torn. A major life decision was not easy. Since I only had enough money to apply to one school, I wanted to be absolutely certain about my choice before putting all my eggs in one basket. But I was so impressed with the knowledge demonstrated on my favorite TV show, G.E. College Bowl, that I decided I wanted to attend the college that won their championship.

When I turned it on, I discovered that the two teams competing against each other on the quiz show that week just so happened to be Harvard and Yale. I didn't choose sides to root for one over the other, but I watched with great interest and an open mind. When the Yale students blew Harvard away by a score of 510 to 35, my decision was made.

Forget Harvard. Yale it would be!

. . .

I walked onto the Yale campus the following fall feeling confident, maybe even a little cocky. I'd won all sorts of honors during high school, made the highest grade in my class for most of the courses, and before making my final college decision, a number of college recruiters had told me how much their schools wanted me.

I expected to impress everyone at Yale.

My first clue college might be harder than I expected came that first week of my freshman year. The other new students sitting with me around a cafeteria table for some reason began comparing SAT scores. Curious, I merely listened at first. What I heard shocked me. Every single one of them had outscored me. And I suddenly realized the Ivy League was a humongous step up from my high school in inner-city Detroit. That should have scared me into working harder at my studies. But it didn't.

In high school, I had always gone to class and read all the assigned materials, but seldom studied seriously until right before a test. Then I'd cram for a day or two and make top grades. That study strategy didn't work so well at Yale.

Still, the possibility of failure didn't sink in until almost the end of my first semester. Each day, each week, I slipped further and further behind, particularly in chemistry (a required course for pre-med majors), which I nearly failed!

By the end of the semester, I had only one faint hope of

avoiding failure altogether. The chemistry prof had a rule: no matter what grades a student had received during the semester, if he/she did well enough on the final exam, the earlier grades would be tossed and only the final counted.

This last ditch opportunity would be my only shot at passing chemistry. So as I opened my chem text to study, I prayed, "Lord, I need your help! I've always thought you wanted me to be a doctor. But I can't stay in pre-med if I fail this class. Please, either let me know what else I ought to do, or perform a miracle and help me pass this exam."

I spent hours memorizing formulas and equations and attempting to read through the extremely thick textbook, trying to understand what I'd not been able to grasp all semester. Finally, at midnight the last night before my final, the words on the page began to blur. I turned off the light, and before I went to sleep, I whispered into the darkness, "God, please forgive me for failing you."

During that night I dreamed I was sitting in my chemistry class all alone. A shadowy figure walked into the dream and began writing chemistry problems on the board. Then the figure worked the problems as I watched.

I woke early the next morning and jotted down those problems, remembering most of my dream with surprising clarity. Then I headed for my chemistry class, numb from exhaustion and the sure knowledge that I was woefully unprepared for the exam.

When the professor passed out the exam, I looked at the first page and saw that question number one was the first problem on the board in my dream. I quickly scanned through the rest of the test to discover the problems were identical to the ones worked out in my dream.

My pencil flew across the pages. I knew the answer to question after question. Toward the end, as my recollection of the dream began to fade, I missed a few. But when I turned in the test at the end of period, I knew I had passed.

After leaving the room, I strolled around the Yale campus for an hour thinking about what had happened and what it meant. I knew God had confirmed that he wanted me to become a doctor.

I thanked him for the miracle he had performed through the dream. And I promised God I would do a better job of using my brain. I would discipline myself to learn how to study throughout a course; I would never again depend on last-minute cramming.

. . .

Another sobering development near the end of my first college semester reminded me how quickly a person's life direction can take a drastic, unexpected, and unavoidable turn. This underscored for me the seriousness of the academic commitment I needed to make.

My brother, Curtis, was the trailblazer for me: as an honor roll student in school; with ROTC; in band. He'd even been Mr. McCotter's lab assistant two years before I was. Growing up, I had always looked up to him as my first role model. If anything, he was more focused and single-minded than I ever was. He never got caught up in the peer pressure foolishness; I have to take full responsibility for my own mistakes there. But the rest of the time, in almost everything else, I was able to see what he did, follow his lead, and use that advantage as a stepping stone in my own journey.

But I did not want to follow in Curtis' footsteps when Congress reestablished the military draft lottery for the first time since the end of World War II. On December 1, 1969, the Selective Service conducted a lottery drawing for young men born between 1944 and 1950, to determine the order of their call for induction into military service during the calendar year 1970.

Each day of each month, from January 1 through December 31, was written on small slips of paper, inserted into 366 blue plastic capsules, and dumped in a large container. With media outlets watching, Congressman Alexander Pirnie of New York reached into the hopper and drew the capsule that held the date September 14. All men born on that date, in any year between 1944 and 1950, were assigned lottery number one and were the first to be drafted and sent to the war in Vietnam.

The drawing continued until all days of the year had been posted in order. Curtis' birthday fell on December 14 and his draft number was twenty-six out of 366. Facing the certainty of being drafted, with the likelihood of ending up in Vietnam, Curtis decided to withdraw from the University of Michigan's engineering program at the end of that fall semester to enlist so he could choose his branch of service.

The U.S. Navy evidently liked his engineering background and trained him for service on nuclear submarines. (By the end of his four years of service, Curtis decided against a career in the Navy and went back to finish his engineering degree.) But during the time when I thought my brother might be headed off to fight a war on the other side of the world, I did some serious thinking about the unpredictability of life, what I wanted to accomplish with mine, and what would be required of me to have the best possible chance of making that happen.

• • •

I had explored such a wide range of new opportunities and challenges that first semester of college. For example, I took a fun course in judo. I found a much higher caliber of chess competition — in the dorm, around campus, and through the chess club — than I'd ever enjoyed back home in Detroit. No matter the hour, someone was always up for a raucous game of

Ping-Pong or foosball. And more people living on one floor of my dorm shared my love of science and similar life goals than I'd ever met—so many potential meaningful friendships!

And do you know how many pianos they had in rooms and lobbies and parlors all over the Yale campus? Not to mention all the practice studios in the music department. A piano had been a luxury we could never imagine, let alone afford, growing up. Even if we'd been given one, Mother could never have paid for lessons. So, with my love for classical music, the university's plethora of pianos provided a great temptation to me that first fall. I'd never had a piano lesson in my life, but before that first semester ended, I had memorized and learned to play the first movement of Beethoven's "Moonlight Sonata."

Clearly, nothing was wrong with enjoying any of these activities. However, the time I spent on them was a major reason why I'd often waited until the last minute to study for my exams.

I had to rethink my priorities.

I'd been having a great time those first few months of college. But my struggles in chemistry, Curtis' draft, and a number of other factors added up, forcing me to put my brain into gear and ask myself: Why are you here?

Carefully considering my opportunity for the first-class education I would be receiving at Yale turned me into a much more serious student for the remainder of my college career. And even the short run. Because I saw so many classmates with tremendous promise (you didn't get into Yale without real potential) who never appreciated the privilege, nor seized the opportunity they'd been given to attend Yale University. A number flunked out before our freshman year ended. Others managed to stick around to compile a mediocre record and an average education.

Another significant potential problem for me, and my fellow students, was something my mother had warned me about during my high school years. She would frequently talk to Curtis and me about the danger of inappropriate entanglements with girls. She seemed to know, as well as I did, how responsible I would feel if I ever got someone pregnant. So I knew she was right when she told me that one such mistake could derail my future plans forever.

Coming to that realization during high school turned out to be a tremendous benefit to me. That didn't mean I couldn't be sociable, but I realized getting into serious physical relationships that early in life could have detrimental consequences. I saw high school friends make that mistake. And sometimes girls would openly and aggressively pursue and pressure us guys, and I'd have to actively, physically extricate myself from the situation.

I was grateful my mother had talked with me about it in high school—because I had so many more opportunities for mistakes in college. In high school I'd be around girls in every class, at lunch, in the hallways. But at the end of the day, they went home and I went home. And even if I went out on a date, she usually had to be home at a certain time and so did I.

College was different. Even at schools that don't allow co-ed dorms or halls (as many colleges do these days), just having guys and gals living on the same campus means temptation is possible and present 24/7. Even back in my day, some girls were so aggressive that they would sit in a guy's lap uninvited and start trying to kiss him and initiate more. I knew to escape those scenarios as rapidly as possible, and that in the heat of the moment there was a real danger of letting my hormones make a decision instead of my brain.

The best strategy was to use my brain ahead of time to make a reasoned and determined decision about what standard I wanted to hold. Better yet, I needed to use my big, creative brain to figure out how to avoid getting into those tempting situations altogether.

The end of my freshman year and my entire sophomore year

of college, my focus was on paying my bills and making the best grades I could. I had little time to even think about girls and dating. Until I encountered Candy Rustin, an incoming freshman at Yale, just before my third year of college.

We met at a reception at the Grosse Pointe Club outside of Detroit, where Yale upperclassmen from Michigan were on hand to welcome incoming freshman from our state. I noticed a pretty young woman with a bubbly laugh. I thought, *That is one good-looking girl.*

When I spotted her that fall, walking across the Yale campus, I stopped her to ask how she was doing in her classes. "I think I'm making all As," she answered. And I thought, *She is one really smart girl.*

Soon, I was looking for her as I walked around Yale, hoping for another opportunity to talk. When she told me that she played violin for the Yale Symphony Orchestra and the Bach Society, I thought, *This is one talented girl.*

* * *

From my first year of college, I regularly attended worship at a nearby church, where the congregation became like a second family for me. I sang in the choir. My roommate and I were often invited to eat Sabbath dinner with families from church. While I didn't ever find a real mentor among my professors while I was at Yale, the choir director at Mt. Zion Church, Aubrey Tomkins, became a mentor and served as a father figure and a spiritual teacher throughout my college career. Since neither I, nor my roommate, Larry Harris, had a car, Aubrey would always drive to campus to pick us up the night of choir practice. Then he'd take us back at the end of the evening, although I don't remember ever returning to campus immediately after choir practice ended.

Sometimes after everyone else had left the church, Larry and I would hang around listening to Aubrey play the piano or organ—sometimes singing along. Often our first destination after choir practice would be Aubrey's home, where we'd listen to his newest records and eat large servings of cake and ice cream. What a treat for a couple of hungry college boys who seldom had money to splurge on anything!

Aubrey loved music, and I learned a lot from being in his choir. But I learned even more from watching him lovingly interact with his wife and children. He provided a wonderful example of what it meant to be a devoted and caring husband and father—a great role model I hadn't had in my life to that point.

My involvement at church was such a big part of my life, that it seemed only natural to invite Candy to visit Mt. Zion with me. Before long, Candy joined the choir there, too. Then we both started going to a Bible study together. We quickly became good friends and would regularly meet after classes to talk. But we were both too focused on school to think about anything more.

For our weeklong Thanksgiving holiday the following year, when I was a senior and Candy was a sophomore, Yale "hired" the two of us to interview Michigan high school students with high SAT scores. The majority of our "pay" came in the form of free transportation back and forth to Michigan in a rental car Yale had booked for us. We celebrated Thanksgiving with our families on Thursday and spent the rest of that week driving from town to town and school to school, meeting with students in the Detroit area who wanted to attend Yale. As a bonus, Candy and I also shared lunch and dinner together every day on Yale's tab.

We left Michigan late Sunday afternoon, planning to drive all night to get back to campus in time to return our rental car as scheduled Monday morning. But we were both already exhausted from the week. Shortly after we crossed the state line into Ohio, Candy fell asleep in the passenger seat.

Cruising along at about one in the morning, I noticed a sign for Youngstown, Ohio. That was the last thing I remembered before I drifted off to sleep at the wheel. The vibration of the tires as they hit the gravel on the shoulder of the interstate woke me with a terrible start. All I saw ahead was the blackness of a deep ravine, and we were heading straight toward it.

I took my foot off the accelerator and jerked the wheel as hard as I could back toward the roadway. The car went into a spin — turning round and round on the highway as a crazy kaleidoscope of scenes from my life flashed through my mind.

I let go of the steering wheel and thought, *This must be what it's like to die.*

When the car finally stopped spinning, it was in the far right, eastbound lane of the highway — the engine still running, pointing in the right direction. I eased the car off onto the shoulder of the road, and a split second later an eighteen-wheeler barreled past.

I shut off the car and said, "We're alive. God saved our lives! Thank you, Lord." Candy had slept through the whole incident but awakened at the sound of my voice.

"Is something wrong, Ben?" she asked. "Why are we stopped?"

I took a deep breath and admitted, "I fell asleep back there, and … I thought we were both going to die."

Candy reached over and took my hand. "The Lord spared us. He must have a plan for us." After that we talked and drove until sunrise to Connecticut. At which point, I eased the car back off the road and pulled to a stop. From then on, we were inseparable. And very much in love.

CHAPTER 10

The Challenge—Medical School

When I graduated from Yale that following spring, Candy still had two years of undergraduate studies to go. I'd applied and been accepted to medical school at the University of Michigan, where I would get a significant tuition break because I was a Michigan native and still an official state resident. Neither of us was happy about the separation, but we vowed to write each other every day. At least I knew I'd be able to see her whenever she came home between terms, during holidays, and over the summer.

I would receive financial aid and be able to borrow enough money to cover most of the cost of medical school. (Lenders figure most doctors are a safe financial risk, which is why many young M.D.s graduate and begin their careers in a huge financial hole.) I didn't want to borrow any more than I absolutely had to, so I needed a job that would earn me some money before I enrolled in med school that fall.

Unfortunately, summer jobs even for Ivy League graduates were few and far between around Detroit that summer. Companies seemed to be laying off workers more than they were hiring. At the time, my mother worked as a nanny for the president of a local steel company. So when she mentioned my predicament to him, he arranged for me to see the personnel director at his plant and I was subsequently hired.

My first day at Sennett Steel, a couple of workmen surprised me when they walked up and handed me a boxy, handheld electronic control unit. In response to my puzzled expression, they grinned. As they leaned back, looked up, and pointed to a huge overhead boom crane hanging from one of many crisscrossing sets of tracks high above the warehouse floor, they explained, "It's what you use to operate that!" After quickly describing and demonstrating the functions of all the buttons and levers to move and manipulate the crane, they instructed me to practice for a while. They'd come back to give me an operator's test on the machine to see if I qualified for that job.

Tentatively, I began to rotate and roll the massive machine back and forth and around the warehouse wherever the maze-like track went. Then I practiced maneuvering the boom up and down. I managed to lift and lower it and move a load of steel. Over the next few hours I slowly trained and gained a feel for this metallic behemoth — or maybe it trained me.

However it happened, when I completed the test later that afternoon, the foreman said, "Well, kid, it looks like you can handle this crane. Be here bright and early and ready to work tomorrow morning."

I was more than a little surprised myself that they would give a job with that kind of responsibility to a young man just out of college with no such previous experience. Since the president of the company didn't know me well at all, I can only assume he must have had incredible respect and trust in my mother.

I got my exercise walking all over that monstrous building, working the hand controls to guide the crane, while maneuvering tons of steel through the narrow passageways connecting different parts of the plant. I also stacked the finished steel products gently onto trucks. The control box boasted more buttons and levers than any modern-day video game controller. I had to work them all in various precise combinations to pick up the steel, balance the load so it didn't tip or sway, then swing the boom over tall stacks of material. I learned how and when to "brake" the crane so the massive machine came to a dead stop at a wall without momentum sending several tons of steel swinging through the barrier and causing tens of thousands of dollars' worth of damage. That crane operator job required an enormous amount of hand-eye coordination on a large, high-risk scale.

By the time that summer ended, I had discovered I possessed a God-given gift to picture things clearly in three dimensions. I could easily visualize just how a multi-ton stack of steel needed to move and where it could fit. What I didn't realize was how learning to think, see, and work in 3-D was a skill I would later require every day as a neurosurgeon operating on a small, high-risk scale.

Part of me hated to see that summer end, because that meant Candy had to head back east to begin her junior year at Yale. Most of our contact over the next two school years would be by letter, because in those days long-distance phone calls cost more than most students could afford. We tried to make the best of the situation and committed ourselves to our studies.

In medical school I followed the rules, went to class, studied, completed assignments, and thought I was doing well. However, it wasn't long before I was disabused of that notion. When I did poorly on the first set of comprehensive exams, my faculty advisor called me into his office to offer what he thought would be helpful advice.

After looking over my records, he told me, "You seem to be a highly intelligent young man, Mr. Carson. I'm sure there are many things you could do outside of medicine."

His words nearly devastated me. The faculty member assigned to provide me advice, encouragement, and inspiration thought I wasn't smart enough to handle medical school and was advising me to go ahead and drop out.

When I told him I didn't want to do that, he suggested the possibility of taking half as many classes, which would require four years to complete the first two years of the program. I didn't want to do that either. So I don't think my advisor was happy when I left his office without agreeing to take any of his advice.

I still believed God wanted me to pursue the dream I'd had since I was eight years old to become a doctor. So I determined to use my brain to think seriously about why I seemed to be struggling and come up with a strategy for addressing the problem.

I'd become a voracious learner since fifth grade; I wasn't going to give up now. The more I thought about how my med school experience was different from the previous twelve years of educational success, the more convinced I became that the issue wasn't whether I could learn (I'd proven that), but how I learned best.

I'd been sitting and listening to lectures hour after hour after hour every day. That was the pattern in every one of my courses, and nothing was sinking in. When I thought back over my previous schooling, it hit me that I had never learned well from just listening. I had always learned best by reading. That meant I needed to come up with a way to use that strength.

The plan I arrived at sounds pretty drastic—maybe even crazy—but from then until the end of medical school, I skipped most of my class lectures. During the hours the other students spent in class, I was in my room or the library reading and rereading the textbook (sometimes more than one textbook) for each of my courses. I studied all sorts of related resources.

I didn't just blow off the lectures; there were "scribes" who sat in every lecture course. These people earned money by taking and typing up detailed notes on every class. I could subscribe to those notes for a reasonable price, and I found I could absorb the material much more efficiently that way than I could by attending the classes. Just before tests, I transferred much of the information onto flashcards for review. Plus, I attended all the labs for the hands-on experiments.

While I would never say med school became easy after that (I studied at least as long and as hard as all the other students I knew), my new strategy began working right away. My grades improved so quickly that I not only shocked my advisor, but I also surprised myself.

. . .

Candy and I continued to write regularly and see each other whenever we could. But we were so tired of our long-distance romance—the long-distance part, not the romance—that we got married the summer after she graduated from Yale. Our wedding was just weeks before I began my third year of medical school—the year med students are expected to choose a specialty and rank the residency programs we hoped would accept us.

So I spent some time analyzing my life direction. I began asking myself, "What is it that I ought to be doing as a doctor? What am I really good at?" Evaluating my gifts and talents was an important step for choosing a career.

I thought, *I excel at things that require hand-eye coordination. I'm a very careful person. I never knock things over and say, "Oops."* I loved to dissect things when I was a kid growing up; if there was a dead animal or a bug around, I knew what was inside. And I had developed a fascination and love for the human brain during all those years reading about and studying psychology. Putting all this together I concluded, *Maybe I should consider being a brain surgeon!*

Initially, I didn't get much encouragement to choose neurosurgery as my specialty. Few people of my racial and economic background pursued neurosurgery. In fact, there had been only eight black neurosurgeons in the world at the time.

I had proven myself in med school and before that at Yale,

but I wondered if I would make the grade in what was often considered the most demanding medical specialty. And I asked myself if a black neurosurgeon could win the confidence and acceptance of the medical community and potential patients.

I went ahead and signed up for two neurosurgical rotations during my clinical years. Receiving honors in both gave me confidence, and the experience I gained during each of those month-long concentrations reinforced my interest about pursuing neurosurgery.

My greatest medical inspiration during this part of my medical training was Dr. James Taren, who not only taught neurosurgery but was also one of the deans and my advisor during my last year of med school. I didn't think of him as a mentor in the same way as I did some of the other teachers who influenced me, perhaps because I was too much in awe of him to feel a strong personal bond. I just felt honored that he knew my name. I respected him because of the high professional bar he set as a brilliant and gifted surgeon and because he was such an admirable man.

Of the countless things I learned from his lectures and from watching him perform surgery, the most memorable lesson didn't seem that important at the time. He had just finished describing what was in those days a controversial, cutting-edge procedure he'd performed on a patient. A med student spoke up to ask, "But wasn't that dangerous? The patient could have died."

"Sure! It was a dangerous procedure," Dr. Taren replied. "But consider the alternative, if we did nothing." It was the first time I ever considered the difficult decisions doctors sometimes have to make—choosing a treatment that could easily cost a patient his or her life, when the patient is even more likely to die if nothing is done. Dr. Taren's words guided and enabled me to weigh the risks in many difficult decisions throughout my career.

Another significant experience during my neurosurgery

rotations started as I watched one of my instructors perform an extremely delicate procedure on a patient. "The hardest part is locating the foramen ovale," he explained as he used a nine-inch-long needle to probe again and again in search of the tiny hole everyone has at the back of the skull.

As I watched this tedious trial-and-error approach to finding this miniscule access point through the bone and into the brain itself, my first thought was ... ouch! This was followed immediately by another thought: There must be a better, less invasive, less painful means of pinpointing the precise location of the spot than poking around in the back of someone's head with a long, sharp needle.

Later that day I stopped by the radiology lab where I had worked the previous summer, and I asked permission to use some of the equipment to do a little experimenting. The challenge was this: Back then the fluoroscopy imaging to see inside the body didn't provide a clear enough picture to find something as tiny as the foramen ovale.

I had an idea that took me a few days to work out. I knew any two points can always be connected by a straight line, so I came up with a hypothesis: I would place one small metal ring at the base of the skull on the back of the head, so that it circled the approximate area of the foramen ovale. Then I would tape another ring on the face at the front of the skull. If I passed a small x-ray beam through the first ring, through the head, and slowly turned and adjusted the angle of the skull until the beam and rings lined up, the foramen ovale should be right on that line.

I performed my initial test on one of the medical lab's skeletal skulls. Then I tried it on a couple of cadavers and easily located the little opening with the needle without having to poke around multiple times to find it.

The process worked so well that I wondered why no one had

thought of it before. However, I hesitated to tell anyone. If I was wrong, I didn't want to embarrass myself. And if I was right, I worried that my instructors, who were all experienced surgeons, might take offense that a medical student would propose a new procedure.

I finally worked up the nerve to tell my professors what I'd done and demonstrated my idea for them. The neurosurgical chief, Dr. Richard Schneider, watched, shook his head slowly, then smiled at me and said, "That's fabulous, Carson!"

None of the surgeons took offense. And Dr. Schneider's response convinced me I was on the right track for neurosurgery.

The human brain fascinated me like nothing else we covered in med school. But we'd barely scratched the surface; there was so much more to learn. I could imagine no greater dream than to become a neurosurgeon. I would be able to improve the lives of others, to not only give them longevity, but also improve their quality of life.

CHAPTER 11

Becoming a Neurosurgeon

Once I'd made my decision to specialize in neurosurgery, I submitted an application for an internship and residency at Johns Hopkins Hospital—perhaps the best and most famous training hospital in the world. But Johns Hopkins usually had only two openings each year for which they received an average of 125 applications.

When I was selected for a face-to-face interview, I made a quick trip to Baltimore, Maryland, for a tour and an appointment with the head of Johns Hopkins Neurosurgical Residency Program, Dr. George Udvarhelyi, who greeted me with a distinctive Hungarian accent.

During the get-to-know-you small talk before the actual interview, Dr. Udvarhelyi, who was also the hospital's director of cultural affairs, after discussing medicine for a short while, happened to mention a classical music concert he'd attended in downtown Baltimore the night before.

I'd attended the same performance since my evening was free the day I arrived in Baltimore. When I told him I'd been there as well, he exclaimed, "You were?"

So we began chatting about the concert. Then we moved on to classical music in general, and for over an hour we discussed different composers and their styles, conductors, orchestras, and even various orchestra halls. Our time ran out before we had the opportunity to return to any medical topics. That didn't particularly bother me, because I knew Johns Hopkins already had all my academic records, recommendations, and so forth required to judge my medical education qualifications. So I felt quite positive about the interview.

Of course, I was thrilled when I received an acceptance notice to Johns Hopkins. As Candy and I celebrated the wonderful news, I told her I wondered if one reason I'd been selected from all those applicants was because Dr. Udvarhelyi was so excited about the prospect of having a resident with whom he could discuss classical music. So my love and appreciation for classical music played a part in getting my residency in my chosen specialty at my first choice institution. (Years later, Dr. Udvarhelyi told me the way I'd handled myself in the interview had impressed him.) That story of my unusual med school interview is perhaps the single best example of a lesson I've been able to share with hundreds of thousands of young people: there's no such thing as useless knowledge, because you never know what little bit of information is going to open doors for you.

After my acceptance into Johns Hopkins' residency program, Candy and I moved to Baltimore. For a time, Candy worked at an insurance company, then she took a job at Johns Hopkins as an assistant to a chemistry professor.

I was putting in such long hours as a resident that I didn't have many hours at home. So Candy used her tuition break as a university employee to enroll in graduate school in the evenings. Before I finished my residency, she had earned a master's degree in business administration and landed a banking job.

During six years of studies at Johns Hopkins, I mastered the basics of neurosurgery and conducted research. By the time I completed my training, the head of my department invited me to stay and serve on the faculty.

But another opportunity arose, and Johns Hopkins was willing to delay my staff appointment for a year.

I had made friends with one of Australia's top neurosurgeons, Dr. Bryant Stokes, when he'd come to Baltimore to celebrate the opening of Johns Hopkins' new neuroscience center. Dr. Stokes and I hit it off so well that he made me a surprisingly serious offer: "Come to my country, Ben, and be a senior registrar [the equivalent of a chief resident in the United States] at our teaching hospital in Perth."

After thinking about the offer, asking professional friends for advice, and praying about the opportunity, Candy and I sensed that God was leading us to Australia. We spent our entire savings on two one-way airline tickets and took off to live 'down under'.

The teaching hospital where I worked, the Sir Charles Gairdner Hospital at the Queen Elizabeth II Medical Center in Perth, was the major neurosurgical center for the entire state of West Australia, which comprises about 1/5 of the continent. So during our one year in Australia I gained more experience using complex and cutting-edge techniques than some neurosurgeons get throughout a lifetime practicing in the United States.

Not long after we returned to the U.S. and I had joined the staff at Johns Hopkins, the position for chief of pediatric neurosurgery opened up. The hiring team could have gotten someone with a big name and a lot of gray hair (and hired him on for big bucks) but they realized that, with my unique training overseas, I could handle the job and for a lower salary. That's how I found myself to be the chief of pediatric neurosurgery at the tender age of thirty-three.

. . .

Less than a year later, I gained professional notice when I operated on a young patient named Maranda Francisco. Her parents had brought Maranda to Johns Hopkins after other doctors had given this four-year-old no hope of recovery. When I first saw her, she was having as many as one hundred seizures each day, despite a heavy regimen of medication. She had almost stopped eating for fear she might choke. She was forgetting how to walk and talk and required constant supervision.

Her previous doctors had noticed her seizures always began on her right side. So they had concluded something must be wrong in the left side of her brain.

So as I discussed Maranda's case with a colleague, we concurred and began to consider a drastic option: a hemispherectomy—the removal of one half of her brain.

This procedure had been performed experimentally some decades earlier, but had fallen out of favor due to serious and often unmanageable complications. We hoped that with current technology and improved surgical procedures, we might have better success. As we talked through it, I became convinced this radical approach was probably this child's best (and maybe only) hope of survival.

But we faced many unanswered questions. If we removed the left half of her brain—the side that controls speech—would Maranda be unable to talk? The left side of the brain controls the right side of the body. Would its removal leave Maranda paralyzed on her right side? Could she live without one side of her brain, or would she die on the table? What if the loss of one side of her brain resulted in damage to the other side? Could we really manage the complications that surgeons had encountered before?

No one we consulted could confidently answer any of our questions. But we all knew that unless we could stop the seizures, Maranda would die.

When I first suggested the possibility of a hemispherectomy to Maranda's parents, they asked, "What will happen if we don't do the surgery?"

I had to answer honestly. "I believe she will keep getting steadily worse until she dies."

Accepting our opinion that the surgery offered their daughter her best chance for life, the Franciscos agreed to proceed. The night before the operation, we prayed, and I asked God to guide my hands and to give life back to Maranda.

The next day we took Maranda into the operating room. Maranda's brain had been so damaged by her seizures that wherever we touched it, the tissue bled. We had to constantly suction away blood so we could see what to do next.

We made one tiny cut at a time, sealed those blood vessels, suctioned that blood away and kept going. It took more than eight hours to separate the left side of Maranda's brain from the right—while I kept praying for God to guide my hands.

Finally, almost ten hours after she was wheeled into surgery, we secured the bone flap back into place.

I followed her gurney out of the operating room and watched while Maranda's parents ran up to see their daughter. When Mrs. Francisco leaned over and kissed her little girl, Maranda whispered, "I love you, Mommy and Daddy." The questions about her speech had been answered.

Then she wiggled on the gurney, and we saw her move her right arm and right leg. And that answered the question about her being paralyzed on the right side.

Maranda went on to live a full life, even graduating from college, with only half a brain. She was only the first of many successful hemispherectomies I performed through the years.

. . .

Then in 1986, I faced yet another, first-in-a-lifetime medical challenge: a chance to pioneer intrauterine surgery—on a fetus still in her mother's uterus.

The case started when I received a phone call from Dr. Phil Goldstein, a Baltimore obstetrician. He had a patient carrying twin girls, one of whom had been diagnosed with hydrocephalus—a condition where cerebrospinal fluid (CSF) accumulates and puts pressure on the brain, causing swelling and tissue death. The affected twin's head was expanding so rapidly that doctors were concerned the mother would go into premature labor and lose both girls. The pregnancy was in its twenty-sixth week, which in the 1980s was too early in the babies' development for the girls to survive.

The best hope for both children was for us to do surgery on the one twin while both of them were still safe, secure, and stabilized in their mother's womb. Such intrauterine surgery had been done on animals, but was considered highly experimental for humans.

The first successful prenatal surgery in the U. S. had been performed in 1981 in California by Dr. Michael Harrison. But in 1986, just weeks before I was presented with the case, the *New England Journal of Medicine* published an article saying that experimental intrauterine surgery was promising but that we had neither the technology nor the knowledge to do that now, and such surgery should not be undertaken until more controlled research could be done.

As I thought it through, I reasoned: If we do nothing, the one twin's head will continue to swell, triggering early labor, and both babies will likely be lost. If we try, the worst result will be that we lose the baby we are operating on. But, of course, we hoped we could save them both.

So Dr. Goldstein and I approached Dr. Robert Brodner, a physician who had developed a shunt he had implanted successfully into animals through intrauterine surgery. The three of us worked on a technique that we felt comfortable trying in the case of these twins.

We arranged to do the surgery at Sinai Hospital of Baltimore. And because of the controversial nature of the surgery, we kept the events quiet from the media.

On the day of the surgery, Dr. Goldstein inserted a large hollow tube, the type used by obstetricians during amniocentesis when they sample the fluid from the amniotic sac surrounding the baby in the mother's uterus. Then, using an ultrasound as a guide, we neurosurgeons took over and ran the necessary instruments for our procedure down through the tube, incising the scalp, punching a small hole through the skull, snaking in a tiny catheter until its tip entered the ventricular cavity deep in the brain. Once that end of the catheter was in place, we set the tiny pressure valve that would open and close to release the excess CSF fluid from the skull and relieve the pressure on the brain. Finally we trimmed and left the opposite end of the shunt dangling just outside of baby's head so that the excess CSF could safely empty into the amniotic fluid that surrounded and cushioned the babies in the uterus.

Our whole medical room team could watch and follow the entire procedure on the screen of the ultrasound monitor placed adjacent to the operating table. Within seconds of inserting and opening the shunt, we could see the baby girl's head begin to slowly and steadily deflate to a more normal size as the CSF drained out. Dr. Goldstein blew out a loud breath, and I exclaimed, "It works! It works!"

We continued to keep a lid on our news, though, waiting to see the outcome after the girls were born. The twins received weekly steroid shots to help mature their lungs in preparation for an early delivery. Three weeks following the surgery, the twins were born by caesarian section. To our delight, both infants moved normally and seemed to be neurologically intact.

Later that day, Sinai Hospital set up a press conference and, with the room filled with newspaper reporters and television cameras, we went public with the news. We had performed the first successful prenatal surgery correcting hydrocephalus. My brother, Curtis, saw the report that night on the CBS evening news and called to congratulate me.

Yet that fifteen-minutes-of-fame experience turned out to be nothing compared to the challenge Johns Hopkins and I received the following year.

German parents Josef and Theresa Binder contacted Johns Hopkins in early 1987 seeking help for their twin sons, Patrick and Benjamin. The boys were healthy in every way, except one: they were conjoined at the back of their heads, facing away from each other. That meant that as long as they remained attached, they couldn't move like normal babies, would never be able to crawl, walk, sit, turn over, or even see each other. The Binders had consulted medical experts throughout Europe, some of whom asked her which twin she would like to keep since both couldn't be saved.

When I flew to West Germany with one of my Johns Hopkins colleagues to meet with the family and examine the boys, Theresa explained that she "lived with a dream that has kept me going. A dream that somehow we would find doctors who would be able to perform a miracle."

They had finally turned to Johns Hopkins looking for their miracle.

Interestingly, I had been speculating about Siamese twins, even before the Binder boys were born. Occipital craniopagus twins—conjoined at the back of the head—are extremely rare, occurring only once in every two million births. And, prior to the Binder twins, no doctor had ever successfully separated such twins without one or both of the twins dying. The insurmountable challenge had always been the loss of blood during the operation because the babies shared so many critical blood vessels. What made this surgery particularly difficult was deciding which twin relied most heavily on which blood vessels and rerouting them appropriately.

As I considered the possibilities, I consulted with a cardio-thoracic surgeon at Johns Hopkins and asked how he was able to operate on babies' hearts without causing a fatal loss of blood flow to the brain. In detail, he explained how he used hypothermic circulatory arrest when doing heart surgery on infants. I had already speculated that if the boys' hearts could be arrested during the most critical stage of the surgery, perhaps excessive bleeding could be prevented. Then the blood could be pumped back again when the operation was over.

After meeting with the Binders, I began to consider the possibility of combining the deliberate cardiac arrest idea with induced hypothermia and circulatory bypass. I wondered: If we could lower the babies' temperatures in order to slow their brain and bodily functions ... and then used a bypass to circulate each boy's blood through a heart-lung machine while temporarily replacing it with saline solution ... maybe we could slow the blood loss enough to give the surgeons enough time to save the babies' lives.

The three techniques had never been used simultaneously for such a surgery. But the more I analyzed and discussed it with others, the more we became convinced this combined strategy offered a reasonable chance to prevent brain damage and give both boys their best hope for a normal life.

I knew, of course, that this approach wasn't merely risky—it meant we would be venturing once again into new, uncharted territory.

Our surgical team spent five months preparing for the separation surgery, complete with three dress rehearsals, each lasting several hours. After each drill, we would discuss each step of the procedure and try to anticipate what problems we might face and how we would handle those possible complications.

On September 5, 1987, at 7:15 in the morning, we made the first incision of the surgery to separate the twins, who by that time were seven months old. As we expected, the boys shared numerous complicated blood vessels that bled profusely as we slowly and carefully attempted to separate them.

We connected the twins to heart-lung machines that circulated blood through the twins as it cooled the temperature from 98.6 to 68 degrees Fahrenheit, thus stopping their hearts. Then, as the blood was circulated to a repository, the heart-lung machines pumped a steady flow of saline solution through the babies' bodies. The saline enabled us to see the anatomy more clearly as we separated the two brains and rebuilt their blood vessels, without the twins bleeding to death.

Twenty-two hours after the surgery began, we walked out of the operating room. And the successful separation of the boys, the first such operation in medical history, made headliners of the Binder twins and earned more renown for the Johns Hopkins pediatric neurosurgery team.

CHAPTER 12

More Twins

My first years as Chief of Pediatric Neurosurgery at Johns Hopkins were filled with a number of historical neurosurgical firsts. The separation of the Binder twins was certainly one of them. But seven years later, I was asked to separate another set of craniopagus Siamese twins.

I received a call from a Dr. Samuel Mokgokong in South Africa. He was caring for Siamese twin girls Nthabiseng and Mahlatse Makwaeba, whose case seemed similar to that of the Binders. He asked if I would consult with him and consider joining his medical team to perform the surgery.

I wondered if a hospital in Africa would have the necessary equipment needed for such a complicated operation. But the Medunsa hospital (MEDical UNiversity of South Africa: Med-un-sa) acquired the special equipment needed: brand-new ventilators (breathing machines), new surgical tools, and state-of-the-art monitors for the anesthesiologists and cardiovascular surgeons. And they arranged to have all the necessary medical personnel: sixty doctors, nurses, and technicians.

That summer, when I traveled to South Africa for the surgery, the Makwaeba twins were sick. The girls' hearts were getting so weak that surgery seemed to be their only hope. If they weren't separated soon, they would die.

The South African doctors and I weighed the risks and decided to proceed with the operation. Using the same combination of procedures as the Binder surgery, we worked to clip and seal all the blood vessels that connected the two girls. At the fifteen-hour mark, they were separated and we pumped blood back into the babies. But the smaller of the two girls quickly weakened and died. Nothing we tried got her heart beating again.

When we finished the operation several hours later, the surviving twin seemed to be in good condition. But within a few hours she began having seizures. Two days later, she too died.

Examining their bodies, we found that the smaller of the two girls had depended on the larger twin's heart. And the larger child had needed her sister's kidneys. They had been completely dependent on each other to live. Even if we had not operated, both girls would soon have died.

What a discouraging case! I had prayed and hoped and believed that God would work a miracle for these children and their family. I wondered why God had allowed me to get involved and travel all the way to South Africa when he had known we had no hope of success. Why had he allowed us to fail?

. . .

In the spring of 1997, Dr. Mokgokong called again to tell me about Joseph and Luka Banda, who had been born recently in Zambia as craniopagus twins—my third once-in-a-lifetime case. Unlike the Makwaeba sisters, Joseph and Luka appeared healthy. Both boys had functioning hearts, lungs, stomachs, livers, and kidneys, and all their major systems seemed to work independently. Unlike either previous set of craniopagus twins, Joseph and Luka were attached to each other at the top, rather than the back, of their heads. So the shape of the connection appeared to be tubular, as if someone had taken a tennis ball in each hand and had mashed them together until the spheres had been compressed.

The extent of the fusion concerned me. How much had the two brains become overlapped and entangled?

When I examined them, I felt where their heads joined and

wondered what problems we would find when we got inside. Rolling the boys gently back and forth, I thought of a way to get some answers to that question.

Months earlier some researchers from the Johns Hopkins radiology department had invited me to their lab for a demonstration. Working in partnership with a high-tech research department at the National University of Singapore, they were developing a 3-D visual-imaging system so that someday surgeons would be able to study cases, examine patients in absentia, and conduct virtual reality surgery by using computerized workstations.

Now, in a hospital on another continent, I hoped we would be able to use this cutting-edge technology in a miracle for the Banda twins. During the next months, Dr. T. K. Lambart, the only neurosurgeon in Zambia, and Dr. Mokgokong collected the data needed—CAT scans, angiograms, and MRIs sent on magnetic tape that could be specially formatted for the research team's virtual workbench model.

It was the next best thing to brain surgery. In a Johns Hopkins research lab in Baltimore, Maryland, I donned 3-D glasses and stared into a small, reflective screen where I could virtually "see" inside the heads of two Siamese twin babies in Africa.

With simple hand controls, I manipulated a series of virtual tools. I could move the image in space—rotating the interwoven brains of these two boys to observe them from any angle. I could magnify the image and examine the small details. I erased outer segments of the brain to see what lay hidden underneath. I isolated small blood vessels and followed them along their interior or exterior surfaces without difficulty or danger of damaging the surrounding tissue. Of course, all of this would be impossible in a real operating room.

The most delicate and time-consuming aspect of the previous surgeries had been the sorting out of overlapping, interconnected, and shared blood vessels. We had to isolate and take down each vessel in the right order—as if we were defusing a bomb. One small mistake could result in brain damage or death.

Being able to study and even memorize the blood vessels around the brainstem, the ventricular system, and the skull base proved an incredible advantage. It was like having a detailed road map of the boys' brains. The chief benefit was knowledge. I noted abnormalities and potential danger areas in order to reduce the number of surprises we would encounter in the real operation.

I arrived in South Africa late on a Sunday afternoon, just after Christmas. Dr. Mokgokong picked me up and took me to the hospital. We met with the members of the surgical team, several of whom had participated in the unsuccessful surgery on the Makwaeba girls back in 1994. We examined our young patients and spoke to the Banda boys' mother.

The night before the surgery, I thanked God for the blessings of that day and asked for his strength, presence, and wisdom for tomorrow. Alone in my hotel room, thousands of miles from home, I prayed for Joseph and Luka Banda, their mother, their family back in Zambia, the medical team—and for myself, asking God to grant me wisdom in knowing exactly what I needed to do during this surgery.

The surgery began at 6:30 a.m. As a result of my practice with virtual-reality surgery, I already knew how the two boys' brains came together and was able to quickly clip blood vessels, in the right order, controlling the bleeding as we worked.

One after another, we isolated, separated and clipped off or reconnected more than a hundred blood vessels. Just when I snipped the last vessel connecting Joseph and Luka, the stereo system that had been playing music in the background of the surgery came to the "Hallelujah Chorus" from Handel's *Messiah*.

After twenty-five hours in surgery, blood was circulating in both brains and neither boy's brain was swelling. Best of all, they had suffered little blood loss, which was the most troublesome part of the previous surgeries. By the time the boys reached the Intensive Care Unit (ICU), both had opened their eyes and were trying to pull out their endotracheal tubes. Even though I didn't know it at the time, there were two reasons why the Makwaeba operation was necessary. One was to make sure that more intensive studies of the twins should be completed before starting the operation, because if we had known how the girls depended on each other for life, we would have proceeded a different way, to hopefully save at least one of them. As long as you learn something from an operation, it is not a complete failure. It was a painful lesson, but we did learn. The other reason why the Makwaeba operation was necessary was to have the appropriate equipment in place for the Banda operation.

Only a few weeks after I returned home, I heard the twins were learning to crawl, something that had been impossible before separation. We had every reason to hope Joseph and Luka would live full and completely normal lives.

. . .

After the media coverage that followed the Maranda Francisco case, then the intrauterine surgery, then the Binder twins, I had felt that my life would settle down again. But each new case, such as the Makwaeba twins and the Banda boys, brought more publicity.

I stayed in the public eye. Life never went back to "normal."

This publicity opened interesting doors for me: newspaper, magazine, radio, and television interviews; speaking engagements at companies, organizations, colleges, high schools, and elementary schools. Over my last twenty-five years as the head of Pediatric Neurosurgery at Johns Hopkins, I probably averaged two speeches a week.

In the schools I visited, I saw trophy cases for all kinds of sports. And I wondered, *Where are the trophies and awards for children who do well in academics? How do we expect children to want to excel in school when athletes are the ones who get all the acclaim and attention?*

So Candy and I founded the Carson Scholars Fund. Carson Scholarships are awarded to students in fourth through eleventh grades who demonstrate both high academic achievement and community service. Each scholar's name is engraved on a large trophy and placed in their school's trophy case. We honor them in front of their peers at school and at regional banquets, and each receives a one thousand dollar scholarship which is invested on their behalf until they start college.

I suspect the publicity from the unusual medical cases explains my invitation to be the keynote speaker at the 1997 National Prayer Breakfast in Washington, D.C. There I had the opportunity to tell my classic dummy-to-neurosurgeon story and discuss my personal faith in God in front of the president of the United States, the president's cabinet, most of Congress, several justices of the Supreme Court, and thousands of other leaders from around the country and the world. What an honor for a kid from Deacon Street in Detroit!

■ ■ ■

In 2003, twenty-nine-year-old Laleh and Ladan Bijani, conjoined twins from Iran, asked their medical team in Singapore to consult me in a surgery to separate them. When they first contacted me, I declined. The risk was too great.

The Bijani sisters were adults and did not have young and adaptable brains. Also, they were healthy and had adapted well, learning to walk together and graduating from college and law school.

But now Ladan wanted to be a lawyer and Laleh wanted to be a writer. They had both gone to law school and obtained degrees, but only one wanted to continue in that career. They searched the world for doctors who could separate them, so each could make her own career choice. Both women insisted they would rather have the surgery and face the possibility of dying than go on living the way they were, with no chance for independent lives.

When I realized the Bijanis were determined to proceed with the operation, I decided to assist their surgical team. I didn't want to wonder for the rest of my life if my experience with previous craniopagus twin cases might have made a difference.

When I flew to Singapore for the surgery, I found Laleh and Ladan to be bright, well spoken, warm, friendly, brave, and very determined to go through with the operation.

Twenty-eight physicians and more than a hundred nurses, technicians, and assistants participated in the surgery. Newspaper, radio, and television reporters waited to hear news of a successful separation.

Thirty-two hours into the surgery, we encountered problems indicating the twins' circulatory paths had changed. Even as we clipped off interconnected blood vessels, their blood found other places to go and other ways to get there. We didn't know exactly what was happening.

I recommended we stop the surgery, sew the women back up, and attempt the separation again later, perhaps in stages, to give their brains a chance to adapt—and give us a chance to study the new vascular landscape. But it wasn't my decision. Laleh and Ladan had insisted they wake up separated or not at all. And the family representative concurred with the twins. I would not have agreed with this, because when you operate, often problems show up during surgery that would not have been foreseeable prior to the operation. Since we had no idea where the blood was going, I told them, you've just consigned them to death. And the hospital and its doctors insisted we go on. After fifty hours, 90 percent of the brain surfaces were separated, and the patients remained stable. Everything looked good.

But the last ten percent was located in the hardest place to reach, a final spot of fused bone that stabilized the base of the skulls and held the two women together.

Unfortunately, in that area, problems began to spiral out of our control. We would clip off one bleeder and another one would start. The twins died from uncontrollable blood loss.

Someone shut off the sound system in the OR. A silent numbness settled over the entire medical team. Tears flowed. After fifty-three hours of surgery, with only three or four hour-long catnaps, I didn't know which feeling was strongest—sadness or fatigue. I just knew it was a horrible feeling I never wanted to experience again.

The media broadcast the tragic news around the world. When I was asked about the failure of the operation, I responded, "It's a failure only if no good comes out of it. I believe a day will come when twins such as these can have a normal life and a safe separation. And I think Ladan and Laleh will have contributed significantly to those individuals in the future who will be able to enjoy what the dream of these two courageous young ladies was—to live normal, independent lives."

The Bijanis were the last craniopagus twin case I ever operated on. But over the next ten years, thousands of other cases challenged our neurosurgical team and me to our limits, and certainly kept my job interesting. I constantly reminded myself that for every one of my patients and their parents—even in the most routine of cases—their surgery would be remembered as one of the most significant, serious, worrisome, perhaps even terrifying days of their lives.

I never wanted it to be routine for me because brain surgery never was for my patients or their parents. While I can't tell you every one of my 15,000-plus surgeries was memorable, I know every one was important.

•••

Those last ten years of my career brought more speaking opportunities than the first twenty. Each spring I accepted as many invitations as I could to speak at high school, college, and graduate school commencements in order to try to inspire as many young people as possible. One school presented my mother with an honorary degree, so she is Dr. Carson now as well. Whenever possible, I've recognized her role in my life by sharing my honors with her.

My family accompanied me in 2008, when I received the Lincoln Medal, an annual award presented by Ford's Theatre in Washington, D.C., that is given to individuals who, through their body of work, accomplishments, or personal attributes exemplify the lasting legacy and mettle of character embodied by the most beloved president in our nation's history, Abraham Lincoln. After a special White House ceremony where I received this honor—along with the first female Supreme Court Justice, Sandra Day O'Connor—President George W. Bush and his wife, Laura, stayed to have pictures taken with the recipients.

When they thoughtfully offered to pose for a picture with Mother, she stepped forward and said she would like a photo with just the First Lady. The president laughed and exclaimed, "I guess I've been asked to step out of the picture!" He was a good sport about it.

. . .

In December of 2012, I informed Johns Hopkins, and made public, my scheduled retirement from the practice of surgery on June 30, 2013.

Many neurosurgeons give up their surgical practice long before they reach their sixties. The fine motor control required to operate on the brain, and the steadiness of hand to work under a microscope making miniscule movements measured in tiny fractions of millimeters, are often the first skills to go as we age. And the endurance required to stand for twelve, fifteen, or more hours a day in an operating room is another physical challenge.

I believed any slight change I might have noticed in my physical abilities was more than made up for by the experience I brought to the operating table. However, I made the difficult decision. Better to give up my surgical practice while I still knew I could go on than to wait until a decline in my skills might endanger my patients. Or to have colleagues begin to wonder whether or not I needed to retire.

Shortly after my announcement, I was again invited to address the National Prayer Breakfast in February 2013. (I felt especially honored when I learned the only other person to do so twice had been the Reverend Billy Graham.)

I decided to share some of the ideas from the bestselling book Candy and I had written the year before, *America the Beautiful: Rediscovering What Made This Nation Great.* A number of my suggestions were quite different from the policies of President Barack Obama, who sat just a few feet from where I stood to speak.

I was surprised by the controversy my talk created. Some critics of my speech thought I should apologize to President Obama for "offending the president" with the suggestions I proposed.

That certainly had not been my intent. In fact, the president and I had a short, pleasant conversation minutes after the breakfast and he gave no indication that he was either upset or offended.

Evidently other people really liked what I said. The *Wall Street Journal* wrote an editorial titled "Ben Carson for President."[2] That certainly hadn't been my intention either.

The demand remained so high that the day after I retired I started crisscrossing the country, giving so many speeches that I went almost three straight months without ever sleeping in my own bed at my new home in Florida. I saw it as a great chance to create a surge of interest needed for the Carson Scholars Fund to take off like never before.

As nice as the public recognition has been, more meaningful are the personal letters I continue to receive every week from people around the world who write to tell me how their lives have been changed by my story. By hearing me speak, reading one of my books, seeing an interview on television or in a magazine, they are being reminded that they have more to do with how their lives work out than anyone else does. Because they too have a brain, they can define their own lives. And if that is the only legacy I leave here on earth, I'll be happy and my life will have been worth it.

---

2. "Ben Carson for President," *The Wall Street Journal,* Feb. 8, 2013, http://online.wsj.com/news/articles/SB10001424127887323452204578292302358207828.

CHAPTER 13

Mother's Influence

It's a strange and humbling experience for me to realize that millions of people around the world know my life story. For some reason, people of all ages, races, nationalities, and backgrounds seem to identify with what I have experienced. They find encouragement and inspiration in the life of a young African American boy born into poverty, abandoned by his father, raised by a single mother, known as the dummy of his fifth-grade class, who eventually became a brain surgeon and head of pediatric neurosurgery at one of the most respected medical training institutions in the world.

Wherever and whenever I've shared my story, I always make a point—as I've tried to do already in this book—of crediting my mother as the single most important human influence on my life. But I want to write a little more than usual here about the Sonya Carson story. She was my greatest inspiration and provided the foundation for everything I've accomplished during my life. She shaped the heart of who I am and taught me eternal truths by demonstrating exceptional character.

Let me share a few examples of what I mean.

Many people praise me for being a role model and an example of someone who overcame terrible hardship in life. Let me tell you, Sonya Carson defined the word *overcomer* for me, because she faced and rose above more hardships than anyone I've ever known.

If anyone has ever had an excuse to be a failure, to just give up on life, or never to think or use her brain—my mother qualified.

Born next-to-youngest of twenty-four children in a family

struggling to survive on a small, hardscrabble farm in rural Tennessee, Sonya knew only thirteen of her siblings. She grew up remembering little about her mother or father, because she spent her childhood lonely and unhappy, being shuffled from one foster home to another.

At thirteen, she met and married my father, a handsome and charming older man who promised to rescue her from her desperately sad situation and take her north to the bright lights and big city of Detroit. My father loved to shower his young wife with expensive gifts of clothing and jewelry. He often introduced her as his "little china doll," and that is how he treated her in the early years of their marriage. My mother was the only person she knew who owned a mink coat. For a while, my father hired someone to come in weekly and clean the house, so his "little china doll" would not be tired out.

My father worked full-time on an assembly line at a nearby Cadillac plant. And he regularly preached at a small storefront church on Sunday mornings. But he didn't always practice what he preached. Years later, Mother told me how my father partied every weekend and how he liked to spend money. One of the things that bothered my mother most was how he always seemed to have all the money he wanted to spend. Yet she couldn't figure out where it came from or where it all went.

Having seldom attended church as a child, my mother did not understand what took place with my father's congregation. Sometimes she felt guilty for not "feeling the Spirit" like others did. She wondered what was wrong with her and why others seemed to be so much more religious than she was.

Growing up as she had, Mother never felt she fit in with any family or any place she ever lived. Now in Detroit, she remained an outsider who seldom felt comfortable in her husband's world. She dreamed of starting a family and finding a role of her own—in which she would truly belong. But whenever my mother talked to my father about having children, he brushed her off by saying, "You don't want to mess up your beautiful figure by getting pregnant. We can have lots of fun, just the two of us. You have me, and I have you. We don't need children."

Finally, after several years of marriage, Mother gave birth to Curtis, and a couple years later, I came along. For the next few years, my mother appeared content with her life. My father seemed to love his two boys and enjoy spending time with our family.

As a young child, I remember understanding that my father's job kept him away a good part of the time. Yet whenever he came home, he was affectionate and played with me and with Curtis. I loved my daddy and thought we had a happy family.

But Mother continued to wonder and worry about where my father was getting his extra money. He spent far more than he could possibly have made working on the Cadillac assembly line and from preaching. She knew something wasn't right. She began to suspect he was involved in something shady — probably gambling, perhaps the illegal sale of alcohol, or even drugs.

Eventually, all those suspicions were confirmed. But the real shocker came when she discovered her husband was a bigamist, with a second wife and children — another family.

When she sat us down to tell us our father would not be living with us anymore, I remember being devastated and confused. By the ages of ten and eight, Curtis and I had to adjust to the sudden reality that our father would no longer play a part of our lives. When my father walked away from our family, he left us destitute. Yet I don't ever remember Mother bad-mouthing him or complaining about her unfortunate lot in life.

. . .

S tarting all over again, Mother fixed her mind and her eyes on a couple overriding goals (although some people would have considered them challenges or maybe even barriers). Goal number one: She determined to do whatever it took to keep a roof over our heads and clothes on our backs, and to provide a happy home for the three of us. Goal number two: Mother proved even more determined to find a way to prepare her sons for achievement and success. She trusted and believed the future would be better than her past or our present circumstances.

From the disheartening new beginning she faced, Mother worked hard to both provide for our basic physical needs and to maintain an emotionally secure home and family life for her sons. Yet she could not always manage to be emotionally healthy or happy herself. The enormity of my father's betrayal and the end of her marriage had been a devastating blow. Suddenly assuming sole responsibility for raising and providing for two young boys must have seemed a terribly daunting task.

Of course Curtis and I were too young at the time to realize how the strain of our new, unsettled circumstances took its toll. So we had no idea why Mother occasionally had to leave us. She simply explained she had to go away for a while to "visit" or "take care" of some loved one. She'd entrust us to the care of relatives or sometimes a neighborhood church lady. She'd usually be gone just a few days, but a time or two, when we lived in Boston with Aunt Jean and Uncle William, she left for as long as three or four weeks. She told us when to expect her back, and she always returned when she said she would. So we didn't worry.

We learned, years later, she suffered terrible depression in those days. And whenever she approached a breaking point, Mother would check herself into a hospital to regain her emotional balance and strength.

Looking back now, I realize what courage it must have taken for my mother to acknowledge and face her own limitations. Knowing what she went through, I have more respect for her than ever today.

Even at that time, I knew my mother's greatest strength came from her faith and the spiritual journey that had begun for her around the time of my birth. During her stay in the hospital maternity ward with me, she met a woman named Mary Thomas, who read Scripture to her and talked with her about God. At first Mother ignored her. When the woman did not go away, Mother suggested that they talk about something other than God.

"My husband is a preacher," Mother told her. "What I know about God is not very good!"

"I do not know your husband," Mary told her, "but I do know God. And He loves you and will never give up on you."

Before Mother left the hospital to take me home, Mary Thomas gave her a Bible. Having only completed the third grade, Mother wasn't literate. Yet she realized if other people could learn to read, so could she. And she determined then and there that one day she would master that skill so she could read this gift from her new friend. That led to another thought, a realization that changed her life: *If other people can do something, so can I. If someone else can do anything, I can too if I make up my mind to it. And so can my sons!*

After her conversations with Mary Thomas in the hospital, Mother began to attend church with her sister Jean (before she and Uncle William moved to Boston). At Aunt Jean's church and another church in our neighborhood, Mother heard, understood, and gradually came to believe more about God—until the day Mother finally dared to say to him, "God, I don't know if I am praying properly. But I now believe you do love and care for me. And I know I need your help." She came away after that prayer with the certainty that God had heard and would indeed help her.

Of course, that is exactly what happened years later when Curtis and I had fallen behind in school, after my fifth-grade classmates nicknamed me dummy, and Mother despaired over our grades and what to do about them. She prayed, and God gave her the wisdom to turn off the TV, make us read books, and require us to present our weekly book reports out loud to her.

One thing we knew for sure was that Mother believed she could turn to God with any and all problems and he would give her wisdom and strength to deal with them.

A year or so after she prayed about our grades, Curtis and I went through a phase of arguing with each other, and sometimes with her, about chores—specifically over whose turn it was to wash the dishes and who had to dry them.

This time, after two days of praying for wisdom, Mother sat us down at the kitchen table to say, "I do the best I can to set up rules around here, but we're having a lot of disagreements lately about chores. Maybe the two of you could use your brains and come up with a plan that would work better than mine."

Curtis and I promised we would think about it, and the two of us soon came to an agreement. We listed all the household chores Mother regularly asked us to do, and a lot of other things she had never expected of us: sweeping or vacuuming the floors; having the dishes washed and the floors clean when she came home from work each night; folding all the clothes; planning meals; cleaning out the refrigerator; and more. We went so far as to set the time and day of the week when we'd have each job done. I imagine our job descriptions surprised our mother sometimes even more than they pleased her. Because she looked at our list of chores, nodded, and offered a big smile as she assured us that, as long as we stuck to our plan, she would no longer tell us what to do. She didn't have to.

Yet she never stopped showing us what to do — by living out essential lessons in front of us every day. Except for that brief period of temporary insanity early in high school, when I fell under the influence of peers, Curtis' and my love, appreciation, and respect for Mother continued to grow — even through our teenage years.

How could they not? Sonya Carson wasn't merely our mother. Even more than our wisest teacher and mentor, she was our steadfast supporter, our loudest cheerleader, our most worthy example, our faithful guide, and our greatest hero.

I will never have time or space to recount all the invaluable lessons I learned from her. Nor would I ever attempt to rank them in order of importance. Mother never made or handed us a to-do list of great expectations; she simply taught us by sharing everyday insights and observations — and by living out an instructive, inspiring example right in front of us.

She knew that in order to provide for her family, she would need to use her brain to gather the necessary knowledge to think things through. So she fixed her eyes on teaching her sons the attitudes that would enable them to use their brains.

She had no doubts that education would provide our escape from the poor side of Detroit. When others questioned the reading and academic demands she placed on us, she told them, "Say what you want, but my boys are going to get an education and be something special one day. They're going to be self-supporting and learn how to love other folks. No matter what they decide to do, they'll be the best in the world at it!"

Once I truly believed that my current circumstances (our family's poverty) were indeed temporary, that learning could indeed provide a way out, that education wasn't some pipe dream, but a life-changing, attainable goal for me, I no longer felt trapped.

Today's frustrating circumstances didn't bother me nearly as much because I had a realistic hope (and eventually confidence) that tomorrow would be not only different, but also immeasurably better. Hope is indeed one of the most powerful forces in the universe. And that gave me a different perspective on life.

The slow, steady, disciplined way she climbed out of her financial hole and the determined manner in which she pursued and achieved the goal of moving her family back into our own home became for me the most memorable demonstration of patience and the reward of delayed gratification. And if that wasn't enough of a lesson to us, Mother's uncanny financial management skills—including her habit of squirreling away enough nickels and dimes to pay cash for a replacement vehicle whenever our current family transportation finally bit the dust—certainly drove home the same point (pun intended; I did grow up in Detroit, after all).

■ ■ ■

Despite the difficult circumstances of her own life, Mother never complained about poverty, hardship, injustice, or any other challenges she'd encountered in life. Nor did she use any of those challenges as an excuse for not doing her best in any endeavor she pursued. She determined that whatever job she had to do, she would do it to the best of her ability. When she mopped a floor, she did not quit until it was as clean and shiny as she could make it. And she held her sons to the same standards.

Because she didn't make excuses for herself, she refused to accept them from Curtis or me. Any attempt on our part to ever blame other people or circumstances for our own failures or misbehavior was a sure-fire guarantee to prompt that favorite question of hers: Do you have a brain? She refused to think of herself as a victim, so she wouldn't let us play the victim card either. And we soon learned that if someone quits listening to your excuses, you quit making excuses. And once you quit making excuses, you can finally begin to use the brain you've been given to find solutions.

Whenever we gave the only possible, positive answer to Mother's brain question, she would often elaborate on her no-excuse, don't-blame-others policy by adding something like this: "Then it doesn't matter what Susan or Robert or Mary or John did or said, you could have thought your way out of that situation for yourself!"

Once, when I felt ostracized and unwelcome by my peers, I voiced my complaint to Mother. She responded by challenging me to use my brain in a different way. "Just suppose," she suggested, "you walk into a classroom or perhaps a school assembly where every other person already there resents you based solely on the color of your skin. They don't want anything to do with you and desperately hope you don't sit down beside him or her. That could indeed make you feel awkward. But it shouldn't and probably wouldn't—if only you took the time to use your brain and consider your 'predicament' from a different perspective.

"No need to worry or feel awkward about your decision. Only those prejudiced folks who are afraid you might sit down next to them have reason to feel worried. So the only awkward predicament is theirs—not yours at all. They have the problem, not you."

My mother's alternate viewpoint was so simple, persuasive, and freeing, that it almost made me laugh. I even gained a measure of empathy and pity for those who would worry that I might sit beside them. That thought-provoking change in perspective convinced me I wasn't the one with the problem and I didn't have to be a victim.

I've always believed my mother's life story to be more remarkable and inspiring than my own. And many people who've heard it and have known her would agree.

Back in 1997, the Mother's Day issue of *Parade* (the weekly magazine circulated in millions of Sunday newspapers around the country) featured Mother in an article telling our family story. They put her photo, accompanied by Curtis and me, on the cover with the article title, "What Mom Knew."

The teaser read: "Sonya Carson missed school as a child, married at thirteen, and was eventually abandoned by her husband. She raised her two boys alone and in desperate poverty. Today, one of her sons is a renowned surgeon, the other a successful engineer."

Judging by the mail in response to the story, Mother finally received a measure of the respect and acclaim she richly deserved. The following year, in a star-studded, nationally televised gala in Atlanta, Georgia, she received the prestigious Trumpet Award given "to inspire, educate, stimulate, and enlighten human minds to the reality that success, achievement, and respect are void of color and gender," presented annually "to men and women who, through consistency and longevity, have achieved success in a chosen profession or career … Potential honorees are those persons who are viewed not only for what they have individually achieved but also for the achievement they inspire in others." Fellow Trumpet Award recipients that evening included General Colin Powell, musicians Whitney Houston and Wynton Marsalis, the Rev. and Mrs. Jesse Jackson Sr., and Deloris Jordan (Michael Jordan's mother).

Having succeeded in raising her sons, Mother continued to think, learn, grow in her faith, and do God's will. She studied, obtained her GED, attended college, and became an interior decorator, specializing in furniture restoration, upholstery, and ceramics.

But the Sonya Carson I know and love considered her responsibilities as a mother to be her primary role. She prepared Curtis and me for our future, taught us how to think, and insisted that we use our brains to help our fellow man and achieve God's purposes.

The greatest mentor I ever had is eighty-six years old. Her own brain is faltering these days as she suffers from Alzheimer's. But she is well-cared for by loving family members and still proudly recognizes Curtis and me, who are forever indebted to her for teaching us, challenging us, and demonstrating for us how to use the brains God gave us to set high goals and pursue our dreams. Before we could ever think much for or of ourselves, she had the determination, wisdom, and faith to think and dream big for us.

Over the years some of my favorite and most frequent audiences are students — from elementary school, junior and senior high, up through college and graduate schools. I love talking to younger people who have so much life ahead of them and so much potential to make an impact on the world. Whenever I address such groups, I always feel a responsibility to challenge them and impart some of those lessons my mother instilled in me — because I've lived long enough now to see what a difference those lessons have made for me.

What she taught and demonstrated for us provided a solid foundation on which to build rewarding and successful lives. I've shared that same wisdom with hundreds of thousands of people around the world, and now I want to unpack it for you in the remainder of this book.

...

Having spent my professional life studying, observing, examining, and operating on brains, I would argue that the human brain is the single greatest, most amazing, immeasurable, unfathomable wonder — not just of the world, but also of the entire universe. And each human being—you, I, every last one of us—has one of these marvels inside our skulls. Not only have we been given such an indescribable gift, but we've also been granted ultimate authority and full responsibility for using it. How we use it is entirely up to us; we can choose the way we think.

To make what has developed into a life philosophy for me as simple and memorable as possible, I've boiled it down to two words. Two words that encompass every lesson Mother tried to convey to Curtis and me. Two words that make worthy marching orders for anyone. Two words that make up the usually unspoken, but only logical, conclusion to that inner dialogue she ignited so often with "Do you have a brain?"

The clear, ultimate implication and application of that truth can be summed up with *think big*. Those letters hardly express all of my thoughts on the subject. Nor do they represent the ranking of importance I'd give each particular point. But this simple acrostic does provide a framework for me to share the most important factors and principles that I know can work as well for you as they have for me. Here are the eight concepts, tied into the eight letters of THINK BIG, which we will cover one at a time in the following chapters:

T = TALENT

H = HONESTY

I   = INSIGHT

N = NICE

K = KNOWLEDGE

B = BOOKS

I   = IN-DEPTH LEARNING

G = GOD

There is nothing I'd rather do for the remainder of my life than to help encourage students (of whatever age) to give their best, strive for excellence in everything they do, and to use that incredible brain God has given each of them to think big enough to change the world by making it a better place for those around them. Because when a person does that, he or she will experience true joy, satisfaction, and fulfillment in life.

CHAPTER 14

Talent

During the years I was deciding what to do with my life, I spent time analyzing myself. I started by asking, "What is it that I really ought to be doing?" That prompted me to also ask, "What am I really good at?" Because no one can adequately answer the first question without thoughtfully asking the second.

I knew I had good eye-hand coordination and that I was a careful and curious person. I loved dissecting things to discover what was inside and how they worked. Once I discovered the joy and benefits of reading, I discarded my self-image as the class dummy and proved to myself and others that I had an excellent mind and could master academic subjects as well as, or better than, my classmates. That early success gave me self-confidence to believe that if I combined effort with my God-given intellect, I could do well in the most rigorous academic setting.

That reassuring conclusion reinforced that unrelenting sense I'd had since the age of eight that God wanted me to be a doctor. By junior high I became fascinated by the human brain. Not just in the physical makeup and workings of the organ itself, but the complex impact it had on all of human existence—what we do, why we do it, how it affects relationships, feelings, and even faith.

As a teenager, I read *Psychology Today* magazine regularly, and that convinced me that we'd barely scratched the surface of all there was to know about our brains. What an amazing mystery it seemed to me!

Then, just prior to med school, I spent that summer as a crane operator moving multi-ton loads of materials around, through, and into tight spots. I realized then that I had the ability to see, move, and think in three dimensions.

As I began med school and continued to think more specifically about what I should do with my life as a doctor, I considered my skills, experiences, and interests. The combination of those things convinced me that I might be uniquely gifted to be a brain surgeon. Except for one serious complication.

In med school I discovered that I didn't (and still don't) particularly like surgery. I have never liked cutting people or seeing blood flow. That part of surgery never appealed to me. The outcome of surgery is what I loved. Knowing I could make a genuine difference in people's lives, particularly the lives of babies and children, gave me great satisfaction.

I also discovered I love teaching people. Being a neurosurgeon at an academic institution like Johns Hopkins, I was instructing someone in almost every surgical situation. So my enjoyment of teaching surgery tempered my dislike of doing surgery.

I found it rewarding to see the people I'd taught move on and succeed in their own careers. I'm reminded of one neurosurgery resident who decided to become a pediatric neurosurgeon. At that time, Johns Hopkins did not have a pediatric neurosurgery fellowship, so he went elsewhere. And there, his instructors were so impressed with him they said, "You don't need to go through a fellowship." Then they made him a faculty member right away.

Even before such experiences affirmed my choice of career, I believed God had gifted me to be a neurosurgeon for a reason. Despite the fact that I didn't enjoy some aspects of surgery, the question I ultimately had to ask myself was: "Should I use the talent God gave me to improve the lives of other people?"

I chose to use my talents; I have no regrets. God tremendously blessed the career he gave me. Now I look back over my years of surgery—all the risks, all the controversies, all the experience, and all the lessons. Then I look at my life after surgery. And I find myself asking a familiar question: "What is it that I really ought to be doing with the rest of my life?" I have a number of appealing options and still have decisions to make. But if life has taught me anything, I've learned I still want to use the talents and strengths God has given me to improve the lives of other people.

I may have retired from surgery, but I still want to think big.

. . .

The first letter—T—stands for *talent*, which God gives to every individual but people seem to define in different ways. If I get the chance, I often ask individuals, "What talent do you have?" They typically respond like this:

"I can sing."

"I can play basketball."

"I'm good at sports."

"I play an instrument."

Most twenty-first century people tend to think of "talent" in terms of sports and entertainment—superstar singers or hotshot ballplayers. Just consider the variety of talent competition reality shows on television in recent years or the number of twenty-four-hour sports channels. We often have a sadly limited understanding of talent.

When I inquire about talents, seldom do I hear someone say:

"I'm good at math."

"I'm an excellent reader."

"I can extract complex concepts from the written page."

"I'm good with computer science."

"In conflict scenarios, I'm a diplomatic person."

"I often tend to think outside the box."

"I have the ability to see needs and then come up with solutions to those needs."

"I have a gift for saying encouraging words to the people around me."

Yet these abilities are talents—invaluable gifts that not every-one possesses. So the first thing we need to do if we're going to think big is to broaden our definition of talent. One simple defi-nition is this: A talent is something that you can do better than other people. But as my choice of career illustrates, I didn't do so based on any one factor or single ability. My combination of skills, interests, personality, character traits, and other God-given gifts equipped me to become a successful neurosurgeon.

Some of those factors that make up the talent to succeed in any career may be less connected to what we can do and more connected to who we are. For example, consider the job of an elementary school teacher. I've met some teachers who were so exceptionally bright that they probably could have excelled in a variety of fields. But many standout teachers worked hard to earn Cs and struggled to get Bs and the occasional A in school.

You don't need to have aced calculus, or even taken it, to be excellent at teaching third-grade math. A mix of a genuine love for children and great patience, combined with an understand-ing of basic mathematics, could make you successful. Indeed, the fact that you were an average student and know what it means to work harder than others could make you especially effective and talented as an elementary school teacher.

So rather than defining talent as "something that you can do better than other people," let's think of it as a combination of somethings—a range of giftings that include innate and learned skills, interests, character and personality traits, intelligence, and acquired knowledge. So each of us is qualified for several, or perhaps a variety of, careers. Just as every human being is a unique and valuable individual, our talent mix can be as distinc-tive as our fingerprints.

We are, in fact, all made in the image of God. That doesn't make us gods—we are not all-knowing, all-powerful, or unlim-ited by time or space. But every human being has some of the character and nature of God designed into us. For example, the types and degrees of human creativity are a reflection of a creator God. We all have at least a little creativity in our nature. Not only artists and actors, but also inventors, builders, teachers, businessmen, landscapers, soldiers, politicians, leaders, software engineers, and farmers exhibit creative abilities.

As a neurosurgeon, I can't study the intricacy of the human brain with its billions of electrical connections without believing in a creator of unfathomable precision and attention to detail. Most human beings reflect some measure of those characteristics in their fine motor skills, but those who exhibit such traits in abundance could use their talents as pharmacists, accountants, computer technicians, and so on. You get the idea.

Then there are divine attributes the Bible calls the fruit of the spirit: love, joy, peace, patience, kindness, goodness, faithfulness, gentleness, and self-control. Being made in the image of God means we have some measure of each of these characteristics, so that these traits/gifts too become part of the mix that composes our talents.

I believe that the ultimate source of all our talent factors is God. If you do believe God is the source of those factors, then whatever fraction of his image, character, and infinite nature that might be, it stands to reason we possess some pretty incredible talent potential—which is the reason we can and should think big.

■ ■ ■

Once we've broadened our definition of talents, we can begin to recognize the various capabilities conducive to success in different careers. Obviously not everyone is capable of doing everything.

An individual could be the smartest person in the world,

but if he has only average fine-motor skills, he won't make a good neurosurgeon. Some people need things concretely laid out, have trouble seeing patterns, and cannot distinguish shades of differences. Such individuals wouldn't make good radiologists, because a radiologist has to be able to note the subtlest of changes.

People-centered individuals would be better suited to public relations, fundraising, marketing, and other careers that call for communicating and personal interaction. Whereas having people skills wouldn't be as essential for an accountant working with numbers or a computer programmer who spends most days writing or translating code.

A language-loving person who enjoys quiet, peace, and solitude would likely be happier as a copy editor or maybe a librarian than a ninth-grade English Literature teacher. Persuasive and verbal skills are a plus in many careers, but they are essential for success in any field of sales. Being an introvert could actually be an advantage as a forest ranger who spends a lot of time alone in the outdoors. The same career could be totally unsuited to an extrovert, unless she also had regular opportunities to guide groups or give lectures and campfire talks.

An ability to think outside the box combined with an adventurous spirit and an open-armed acceptance of change could serve an entrepreneur or an inventor well. Individuals whose personalities tend toward ADHD are going to be happier and more successful in a career with a variety of responsibilities and perhaps a high degree of unpredictability. The very opposite of what you would look for if you like to concentrate and persist on tasks until they are done.

I know some intelligent individuals who just do not have the ability to form a good oral argument. They know what they want to say but can't translate their thoughts into appropriate words. If they stick with it, they may get their point across, but it takes them a long time and too much energy. They would not be suited for a career as a trial lawyer. Yet they could have a logical mind and problem-solving abilities that would prove a strength in any engineering field.

The possible combinations are practically endless. Thinking in these terms and beginning to see connections is the first step in discovering and recognizing your personal talents. When you understand the range of giftings, it's time for serious self-assessment.

I started this chapter mentioning some of the factors in my own life that eventually convinced me that my combination of skills, personality traits, and interests added up to convince me to say, "I should be a brain surgeon."

Perhaps I could have become a lawyer or an engineer like my brother, Curtis. I had the reasoning and communication skills required of the first, and the mathematical aptitude for the second. But I don't think I would have excelled in either of those areas in the same way that I did in neurosurgery. I wouldn't have taken advantage of nearly as many of my personal strengths and interests in any other field; I'm convinced I made the right choice and found the perfect talent fit for me. No regrets.

Let me emphasize that it was a choice. Anyone with a normal brain has a resource so fantastic that they have the intelligence necessary to take on any number of careers. But when a person identifies, develops, and uses his own unique talent, he is likely to excel. Then he can wisely choose careers that allow him to maximize as many of his giftings as possible. Doing that takes time.

For instance, Johann Sebastian Bach probably had what it would have taken to become a doctor (there is a strong correlation between science and math and musical aptitude). But had he done so, he couldn't have taken maximum advantage of his talents as a musician, and we wouldn't be able to enjoy his music today.

I found self-analysis to be the most effective way to identify my own talents. I'm convinced it's invaluable for everyone. (If you're ready to begin your own self-assessment of gifting and talents, I'd suggest you look over and answer the questions in the exercise "Personal Talent Assessment" at the end of this book [page 227]. (Taking a few minutes to work through questions 1–5 right now could prove helpful as you continue reading.) But there are other ways to explore or to validate your own judgment. Do your research to see which tests are most reliable:

- Standardized personality tests can identify underlying character traits.

- An aptitude test could reveal a pattern of traits or tendencies, which, if combined and developed, could lead to career choices you'd never seriously considered.

- Guidance and career counseling offices in high schools, colleges, and grad schools may administer both kinds of tests, or you could take them online.

I hesitate to endorse guidance and career counselors too highly, because some give bad advice. If I'd listened to my first advisor in medical school, I would never have become a doctor. Use such people for more general knowledge and advice about testing, educational requirements, schools, and options. Continue to do your own analysis and make your own decisions on what talents you will pursue and develop.

Then seek more opinions. For as Proverbs 11:14 says: "Where there is no counsel, the people fall: But in the multitude of counselors there is safety" (NKJV). I suggest you limit the "multitude" to people you respect and trust and who know you well. Use them as a check-and-balance with your own analysis.

I offer that caution because I've seen too many cases where people have placed too much stock in others' opinions and came to regret it. Here are two common scenarios where that can happen:

First, your parents may end up guiding you into areas for which you may have neither interest nor talent, and have little chance of being successful or finding fulfillment. While I always encourage respecting and listening to your parents' guidance, you should be open to others' opinions as well. Immediately, I think of my friend and former colleague, Hamilton Moses III (his friends call him Chip). His great-grandfather, grandfather, and father were all Harvard-trained lawyers. Quite naturally, the family fully expected Chip to follow suit. He did go to Harvard but bucked the system by pursuing medicine instead of law, which created a considerable and unhappy stir in his family. This man stood against family expectations to use his giftings and became a talented physician who went on to be one of my bosses as a vice president of Johns Hopkins Hospital.

Second, even if you are blessed with celebrity-quality potential and talents as popularly defined by sports and entertainment, you may need an extra-strong tether to reality. You may be such an impressive athlete that your family, friends, and even coaches say, "You have what it takes to make the pros." Or people who've watched you sing, dance, and/or act may tell you they "just know you're going to be a big star someday." But your chances of reaching the top in the glamourous fields of sports and entertainment depend on factors other than talent—such as timing, connections, health, opportunities, coaches, and teachers. The right breaks at the perfect time, an unexpected occasion to impress, what most people would call pure luck. Your chances of success in large part depend on factors totally out of your control.

Only three out of every ten thousand boys who make their high school basketball team ever make the NBA. The odds of success in the entertainment world can't be much more promising.

You'd be foolish to head down either road without first doing the necessary self-analysis of all your talents and thinking through the possibilities enough to have some alternate, back-up plans.

. . .

The secret to developing talents may be simpler than identifying yours and choosing which careers you'll pursue. The first requirement is something we each have the same amount of every day: time. Time is essential to almost every aspect of the THINK BIG concept.

I didn't emphasize how much time it took me to decide that my collection of talents could serve me best as a neurosurgeon. I considered, thought, talked, explored, and prepared—over years. It takes time to know yourself well enough to make a confident choice.

Most people spend more time planning what they are going to do for their birthday each year. It doesn't matter how old you are; invest time in self-analysis of your talents. You also need time to develop those gifts, traits, and abilities in ways that will bring success and provide an opportunity to impact and improve the lives of others around us.

What we do to develop our talents is as important as the innate potential we were born with. Recent studies suggest that it takes ten thousand hours of effort, work, practice, etc. to develop a world-class talent at anything—from baseball to violin to chess to computer codes. (More about this in Chapter 20, when we talk about In-Depth Learning.) That means that we don't practice because we're talented at something, but rather we must practice something (a lot) to develop that talent. And there's nothing to keep us from continuing to develop our talents throughout our lives.

There is no reason why most of us can't be world-class experts at something we enjoy doing. That could happen if more people would learn to think big, which has to start with identifying, developing, and then using our talents, because there is no real point in identifying or developing our talents unless we're going to use them.

As a result, I'm a big advocate of using our talents as early in life as possible. There's a good chance we might identify and begin to develop others in the process. That was certainly the case for me. Both my first "work" experience as a volunteer lab assistant, then my first paying job as a college lab assistant enabled me, while still a high school kid, to begin learning and developing basic science and lab skills I used throughout my career. And my crane operator job, which had nothing to do with medicine, provided me the chance to discover my aptitude for three-dimensional thinking. Every other part-time job I had through college and grad school helped me learn at least some basic work skill that anyone needs to do a better job at anything.

God gives every human being the capabilities each of us needs to make a contribution to the world. Most of us have a variety of options. But if we're going to find a real sense of purpose and fulfillment by making life better for the people around us (and how much bigger could we ever think than that), we all have some thinking to do and some choices to make.

CHAPTER 15

Honesty

One of the earliest and most embarrassing lessons I ever received on honesty occurred while our family lived with my aunt and uncle in Boston.

I suspect Aunt Jean had a serious sweet tooth, because she kept a private stash of candy bars partially hidden in the back of one of her kitchen cabinets. She regularly spoiled us with all sorts of treats, but even without being told, Curtis and I knew that the big box of candy bars was Aunt Jean's. They weren't ours for the taking.

We knew we needed to wait for our aunt to offer us one. But it was all too tempting for two young boys to think: There is almost an entire box of candy bars in that cupboard. Aunt Jean won't miss just two. She probably doesn't know exactly how many are in that box. Even if she does keep count, she wouldn't really care. She's always so generous with us ...

Curtis and I each took one, ate the candy bars, and carefully disposed of the wrappers.

I never knew how Aunt Jean found out. Perhaps she did keep track of how many candy bars she'd eaten and how many remained in the box. Or maybe she knew little boys well enough to read the guilt on our faces. Somehow she knew. And I'd never felt worse or more repentant than I did when she confronted and scolded us for taking those candy bars without permission.

That sense of shame was nothing compared to what I felt when Aunt Jean informed our mother what had happened. We had to endure an even more pointed tongue-lashing from her. She reminded us that we not only knew what she expected of us, but we also went to church every Saturday and knew what God expected of us.

"You know, boys," she wanted us to realize, "this is Aunt Jean, who has sacrificed for us, who took us into her home after the divorce. And how do we repay her? By stealing her candy bars?"

The implied message being that if we had spent just a little bit of time thinking, surely we would have come to a different conclusion and behaved differently. While mother wanted us to recognize how our behavior had demonstrated ingratitude toward our aunt, the primary message about honesty also came through loud and clear.

No doubt my memory of the candy bar episode played a part in another incident that took place a few years later.

One day while I was at the grocery store, the cashier handed me my change, and as I headed for the door I realized that she'd given me a ten instead of a one-dollar bill. As I walked out of the store, I began to fantasize. What can I do with my extra nine dollars?

By the time I reached home, I had a knot in my stomach the size of the fist in which I still clutched the money. And I was no longer rejoicing over my "good fortune."

I did not mistake what I was feeling. I knew it was guilt. And I knew keeping the money wouldn't be honest.

So as soon as I put the groceries away, I walked back to the store where I returned the ten-dollar bill to the clerk and explained what had happened. She gave me the correct change, and I strode out of the store nine dollars poorer but feeling on top of the world.

That experience reinforced for me an even more important truth than the virtue of honesty. It reminded me that there is such a thing as right and wrong, and when you do what is right, based on the principles you believe in, the satisfaction that results is better than having money.

When it came to honesty, truthfulness, integrity, and doing the right thing by others, Sonya Carson had set the bar high for us. No one can hope to think big and achieve meaningful success in life without considering and factoring in the issue of character. In fact, I've been encouraged in recent years to see how many schools—from elementary through graduate schools—have made a conscious decision to add or incorporate values and character education into their academic curriculum with the goal of teaching, developing, and strengthening the character of their students.

■ ■ ■

As a personal goal or standard for character, the definition of honesty covers a lot of territory for most of us. Certainly, it means telling the truth. But it also means: treating others fairly; choosing to do the right thing; admitting and taking responsibility when you do wrong; and demonstrating integrity.

Mother always found work, despite her limited job skills, because the people who hired her quickly learned they could trust her—in their home, around their valuable possessions, and with the care of their children. She gave them their money's worth by giving her best at whatever she was asked to do.

In her mind that was all part of treating people fairly, doing the right thing, and demonstrating integrity. That was the way she lived, and it was the way she expected us to live, and the way she expected others to treat her.

I remember riding with mother one day when a man in the car behind ours bumped into us. Although we weren't hit hard enough to be injured, the blow felt like it could have put a dent in the bumper or the back of our vehicle. Mother quickly checked to make certain I was okay and then started to get out to talk with the other driver. But by that time, the man was pulling around us and driving away.

Mother yanked her door closed, shifted into drive, and took off after the guy. I didn't know what in the world my mother planned to do if she caught up with the hit-and-run culprit; she looked more determined than she did angry. We were in Detroit, so the guy we were following couldn't stomp on the gas and roar away from us on the open road. The traffic and traffic lights kept him within sight until we could catch up. No matter how many turns he made, mother stayed right on his tail. We chased him halfway across the city before he finally gave up and pulled to the curb.

She made me stay in the car when she got out to get the man's insurance information, so I don't know what all my mother had to say to that driver. But before she finished giving him a talking to, he appeared to have learned an honesty lesson that day, about doing the right thing and taking responsibility for your mistakes. And I learned more about how important honesty was in my mother's eyes.

By the time I left home for college, I might have said honesty was just as important to me. But the proof of my convictions was demonstrated in a couple of experiences at Yale.

I landed good jobs and worked hard to earn money every summer of my college career, but by the time I paid for basic school supplies, laundry, assorted fees, and other incidentals, I had little money left to get me through the school year. Once during my sophomore year, I was so broke that I was praying as I walked across campus, *Lord, please help me. I need at least enough money for bus fare to get to church.*

As I neared the old college chapel, I looked down and spotted a ten-dollar bill lying on the ground. Thank you, Lord!

During my junior year, I hit a similar low point — not enough money for bus fare or a phone call. Remembering what had happened the prior year, I set out on another walk across campus toward the chapel, praying and looking on the ground for money the entire way. But I found nothing.

That same day I had to retake a test. According to a posted notice, the exam papers from a psychology test I had taken a few days earlier had been "inadvertently burned." So I headed over to the classroom in the psychology department to take the test again.

The professor distributed the exams to the one hundred fifty or so students and then walked out of the room. When I began reading the questions I thought, *Whoa! These are much, much more difficult than the questions on the original test!*

Evidently, I wasn't the only person who thought so. After a moment, another student spoke up. "Can you believe this? I can't answer these! They're too hard! I'm leaving. I'll tell the professor that I didn't see the notice about the retest. They'll have to offer the test again, and I'll know what to study the next time." With that, the student stuck the test in his bag and left the classroom. Soon other students decided to do the same thing.

After reading through all the questions, I just sat and stared at the test. I knew I'd done well on the previous test; I had no idea how to answer some of the new questions. It wasn't fair! *But I have to try and do my best*, I thought. *I won't lie and say I didn't see the notice.*

So I kept working, occasionally hearing other students get up and walk out. A half hour later, I was the only student left in the room.

Suddenly, the door swung open and the professor walked in. With her was a photographer who walked over and took my picture.

"What's going on?" I wanted to know.

"A hoax," the professor replied, smiling. "And something of an experiment. We wanted to see who the most honest person in this class is. And you won!"

Then the professor handed me my reward: a ten-dollar bill. Sometimes honesty pays! Actually, I've since realized honesty always pays—at least in the long run. But that day it paid on the spot. With a ten spot. In a bad spot—when I really needed it.

Another lesson about being honest I learned was from someone who wasn't. One of my brightest classmates at Yale graduated magna cum laude. To do that, he had to make As in almost all of his classes for four straight years. But he was not trustworthy or honest. He routinely broke curfew and often had women in his dorm room overnight (which wasn't allowed in those days).

He also cheated on tests, even though he was intelligent enough not to need to. Yale used an honor system in testing. Professors would hand out their exams and often leave the room while students completed them. During our exams, I saw him open his book and look up the answers to questions on several occasions. Other students noticed his behavior, too.

Rules were a joke to him or challenges to overcome. Disobedience seemed like a game. He never demonstrated any guilt or embarrassment about his behavior.

Even though he graduated with honors, of all the pre-med students I knew at Yale, he was the only one who wasn't accepted into any medical school.

His fellow students saw what kind of person he was. Evidently, to his surprise, so did his professors—which was no doubt the reason he didn't get the faculty recommendations he needed to get into med school.

I lost track of him after we graduated. So I don't know if he ever learned anything from his experience. But what happened to him convinced me that people who think they are hiding their dishonesty, who believe their misbehavior will go unnoticed and won't negatively impact their lives, are always deceiving themselves.

. . .

Honesty means a lot more than not stealing other people's possessions, not taking advantage of someone else's mistake for your own benefit, or not cheating in school. It's not merely defined by what you don't do, but also by what you consistently will do. Some years back, when I faced a situation involving a sum of money far greater than grocery store change, I learned that honesty sometimes means remaining true to your own beliefs and values even when that requires sacrifice on your part.

I had signed a contract to coauthor a book about specific health problems from which African Americans suffer in even greater numbers than the general population. Many of these health problems—heart disease, stroke, hypertension, certain types of cancer, and so on—can be greatly affected by lifestyle choices. So our book suggested practical and specific everyday changes. But the publisher complained of too much moralizing for a book on "medical issues."

For example, in a discussion of sexually transmitted diseases, I suggested abstinence was a highly effective and reasonable means of combating the problem. I even suggested that any young man who was thinking about getting into a sexual relationship should ask himself, "Would I want someone to do to my sister what I plan to do with this woman?"

The publisher considered my promotion of abstinence moralizing and did not want to include it for fear it would offend readers.

I refused to take it out of the book. I made that stand not only because I felt it was valid medical advice, but also because it reflected my own strong convictions. The publisher refused to publish the book, and I had to return the money I'd been paid upon signing the contract. I was simply not willing to compromise my principles and publish a book simply for monetary gain.

The decision was unpleasant, because I had already invested a lot of time in the book. But the decision was not difficult, because I believed, and still believe, such choices should be based on principles. And that belief is founded not just on my mother's teachings, but also on the wisdom of King Solomon, the wisest man in the ancient world who wrote in Proverbs 22:1, "A good name is more desirable than great riches; to be esteemed is better than silver or gold." Honesty, integrity, and being true to your own principles are the surest way I know to establish a good name.

Sometimes keeping a good name can be as challenging as earning one in the first place. I learned that during a thorny predicament several years ago when I was invited by a Maryland right-to-life group to tape a television commercial for their cause. Since I have made it a priority to try to preserve rather than take life, I happily agreed to help.

My television commercial drew much positive response. But as the weeks passed I noticed something that began to bother me in the overall campaign to persuade voters to end elective abortions in Maryland. Some of the information distributed, and some of the arguments being made, were not entirely accurate. The more I saw of what seemed like scare tactics and misleading statements in this campaign, the more uneasy I felt about my name being associated with it. So I called the group's headquarters and asked that my commercial be withdrawn.

Considerable public debate resulted when word of my decision leaked out. Many people concluded that my employer, Johns Hopkins, had forced me to recant my position. But no one ever did, or would have done, such a thing.

The decision was only difficult in the sense that I did not want to hurt a cause I believed in by withdrawing my public support. Making the decision itself was easy enough — because I saw it as a matter of principle. I believed there were plenty of valid arguments and excellent reasons for me to oppose abortion, but if I wanted to stand for the principle of truth, I needed to be consistently honest in the public stances I took. I could not in any way allow my name to be publicly associated with statements that were only partly true and, therefore, misleading. It was as simple as that.

Of course, we all make mistakes and fail to live up to our standards and principles from time to time. When that happens, we need to admit our mistake, apologize, and do whatever we can to repair any damages done, reconcile relationships, and make the wrongs right. The quicker we do that, the faster we regain our integrity. Having high standards of honesty and truthfulness won't mean we'll ever be perfect in everything we say or do. We are all human. But a reputation for each of those traits can be achieved with

- a good-faith effort to set and pursue those standards
- enough humility to admit our inevitable shortcomings (to ourselves and others)
- the faith to consistently press on with a desire to do better in the future with God's help

Consistency in character, as in almost everything else, usually becomes easier with time and practice. But experience has taught me that investment nearly always pays off in the long run by making life simpler and more predictable.

I was reminded of that by a shocking phone call I received one day while I was in the middle of brain surgery on one of my patients.

When the phone on the operating room wall began to ring, one of the nurses went to answer. I heard her say, "Dr. Carson's here, but he's in surgery at this moment. Do you need to speak to him?" There was a pause before she said, "Just a moment; I'll see."

As the nurse walked toward the operating table with the receiver in hand, I asked who was on the line. When she gave the name of one of the hospital administrators, I nodded my permission, and the nurse held the phone up near my ear while being careful not to touch me and contaminate the sterile field. My caller apologized for interrupting, but said he'd just been contacted with information he thought I should know about immediately. He told me the hospital had just received notice from a court in Florida that a woman, whose name I had never heard before, had filed a court claim naming me as the father of her child. I assured the caller I was absolutely, 100 percent certain the charge could not be true, but that once I finished my Operating Room schedule for the day, I'd come by his office to get further details. I thanked him for calling and calmly, confidently went back to work on my patient.

I could do so because I had set my standard for sexual behavior high, and I'd consistently abided by that standard. Since I knew for certain that my wife, Candy, was the only woman I'd ever slept with, I didn't have to rack my brain and wonder if I'd somehow slipped up and could possibly be guilty of this charge. Being the subject of a paternity claim was certainly annoying. And I realized it might be embarrassing if word got out and people believed it. But since I knew the accusation couldn't possibly be true, I felt certain that nothing serious would come from this claim.

And it didn't. According to this woman's claim, she'd had a sexual relationship with a Dr. Benjamin Carson she claimed was living in Atlanta, Georgia, during the time I was doing my residency at Johns Hopkins in Maryland. My lawyers got a statement from Johns Hopkins indicating that was impossible because

I had been required to live within thirty minutes of the hospital at the time. We also demonstrated that every one of the "personal details of my life" this woman listed as proof of her relationship with me could have been gleaned from one of the many magazine or newspaper articles written about me in the wake of one or more of my most publicized cases.

The judge immediately dismissed the case for lack of evidence. The woman had to pay the court costs. And I never heard from her again.

Let me wrap up this subject by summarizing what I usually say about honesty when I speak to students in schools around the country. If you want to think big, be successful in life, achieve something significant, the "H" needs to be key in your life philosophy.

If you live a life marked by honesty, truthfulness, and integrity, you will never have to worry about any skeletons in your closet. Because if you put them there, no matter how long ago, they will come back to haunt you for sure.

And if you always tell the truth, you will never have to struggle to remember what lies you told to whom three months or three years ago. Life is so much simpler that way, which makes it that much easier to concentrate on the task at hand—using the brain God gave you.

CHAPTER 16

Insight

When I was growing up, we established a family tradition of "bringing in the Sabbath" at the end of each week. Mother, Curtis, and I would gather in the living room. We'd begin by reporting and discussing what had happened to each of us, good or bad, during that week. Then Curtis and I would play our instruments while Mother would sing. And finally, we would read from the Bible and pray.

With two years between me and my brother in school, plus our mother's long hours spent working each week, we could have been a trio hearing and singing different tunes while living separate lives out of the same house. But this weekly tradition became a touchpoint where we regularly connected as a family. Those evenings were my opportunity to learn about and react to all that had happened to my mother and Curtis that week, and for me to share and hear their perspectives on my experiences of the week.

Those evenings were my initial exposure to the wonderful concept represented by the first "I" in THINK BIG: *insight.*

Insight is the ability to learn from observing and experiencing life. And to use that acquired knowledge to discern truth, principles, and lessons you can apply to future relationships, situations, and decisions—thereby gaining wisdom.

Mother and Curtis frequently looked at the events of my week so differently during those conversations that I soon learned there was usually a different perspective, often a good one, to consider. I was struck by how often Curtis and Mother noticed different details, attached different meaning, drew different conclusions, and took away different implications even from shared experiences.

I particularly remember one Sabbath discussion after a friend had asked to borrow my bicycle. I saw no reason not to loan my bike to a friend—until I shared that possibility with my family.

My mother asked me, "Doesn't he have his own bike?" He used to, but it had been lost or stolen.

"What happened to that person's bike? If they didn't take proper care of their own bicycle, Ben, why do you think they will take care of yours?" Good question.

I hadn't factored that into my thinking. Mother talked to us a lot about taking care of our stuff so that we didn't have to spend money buying replacement stuff. And we'd certainly seen her practice what she preached with her own things. I just hadn't applied that principle to my bike situation. But with that relevant insight, I decided against letting my friend use my bike.

Those family times frequently included what we'd done that week that had positive outcomes, as well as disappointing experiences. We'd consider the choices or actions that might have contributed to less-than-desirable outcomes. I can't say I always appreciated the differing perspectives, but I eventually gained some valuable insights about cause and effect.

· · ·

We are not born with insight. But every human being has the capacity and potential for insight. We can nourish and develop it—and we need to if we're ever going to think big successfully.

Insight happens in that moment when you cry out "Aha!" or "Eureka!" (which literally means, "I've found it"). You can't schedule it, or confidently anticipate its time, or even method, of arrival—because insight may come suddenly at light speed or slowly. And it enters through many doors:

- From our own life experiences when we ask ourselves the right questions
- Through mentors who have already gained success
- When we read and learn from the mistakes and achievements of others
- As we avoid the common mistakes of following our peers

One insight came at a critical point for me: my academic struggles during that first semester of med school, when my advisor thought the most reasonable plan for my life would be to drop out, forget about becoming a doctor, and find another profession. I was devastated and at a complete loss as to what I should do. But since I firmly believed that God wanted me to become a doctor, I prayed and asked him for insight. Then I began to review all the learning experiences of my life.

When had I struggled; when did I flourish? Which classes had been hardest, which others a breeze? How did I learn best and how did that vary in the answers to the previous questions? I looked at my personal academic history from every angle I could think of—until I was struck by the great bulk of the empirical evidence that pointed to an undeniable fact: Not only had I first discovered I could learn by reading, but since fifth grade all the way through college, I had learned more by reading than any other way.

When teachers and professors had lectured, I would listen carefully and take notes. But it wasn't until I read the notes that I fully grasped the lecture material. When it came to mastering any subject, reading was the most effective and efficient modus operandi for me.

Once I realized that, the question became: how in the world can I apply this insight to my situation? After six or eight hours of lecture each day, I'd often spend about the same amount of time each evening reading and trying to process that day's notes so I could keep up. After that, I spent more long hours with my textbooks and other reading materials in preparation for each class the following day.

All those lectures ate up a huge chunk of each day. And there never seemed to be enough hours at night to make up for it.

That insight gave me the confidence and conviction needed to execute one of the most drastic, and seemingly crazy, decisions of my life. A few of my classmates questioned my thinking when they first realized I showed up for each of my labs but skipped all the lectures, purchased class notes to review later, and spent all my newly salvaged hours reading and absorbing the boatload of knowledge thrown at us, the way I'd always learned best. Our lecture classes were all so large, I don't know that any of my professors even noted my absence. If they did, their concerns — like the questions of my classmates — were put to rest as my grades soared upward and stayed at or near the top of my classes the remainder of the year.

Nobody else recommended that strategy. I doubt anyone ever would have. But it turned out to be one of the most important and wisest decisions I ever made. Insight springing from my own observations and experience led me there.

Insight also played a major role in my decision to do that first hemispherectomy. I knew that Maranda Francisco's life hung in the balance. So I went back and looked at what many other people had said about previous efforts to do this surgery. I asked myself some pertinent questions. What had led to that operation falling out of favor? Is it still a problem? Or is it something we now can potentially solve? Is there new technology that makes the operation work better?

The answers to those questions gave me the insight and the courage I needed to try a radical surgical approach that saved a little girl's life.

Asking the right questions is essential to gaining insight or solving any kind of problem. We want to make decisions based on facts.

Many people do not. They make their decisions based on what their momma says or what their daddy says or what their political party says—without engaging their brains.

Instead, there's something to be said for asking yourself these questions: "If I do this, what happens? And what happens fairly consistently every time I do this? What does that mean? What are the implications?" That's the empirical learning method used in science and math.

■ ■ ■

We can also learn from the mistakes and the achievements of others.

My mother was my first mentor and my richest source of insight growing up. I've told you how she observed and learned from her experience in the homes of her wealthy employers. She noticed everything about their lifestyles: what activities they participated in, how they spent their time, and even what they read. She made the comparison between how hard they worked and the behaviors of so many of the people living around us. That insight gave her the motivation to work twelve to eighteen hours a day to stay off welfare, to decide education was the surest and best way out of poverty for her sons, and to believe that our lot in life would improve someday.

Mother also noticed her employers' clothing and saw how they selected clothing of quality. She heard them say, "You get what you pay for." She observed and learned that the better-quality clothing did indeed wear better and longer. We could not afford many new clothes. And there was no way we had the money for the top-of-the-line, name-brand quality her employers owned. But Mother learned to find more durable, better quality used clothing at resale shops. Even if she had to spend time altering the clothes on her sewing machine.

I hated shopping in thrift stores with her for fear that my friends might see us buying used goods. I would have been embarrassed for others to know that we wore used clothing. But that never seemed to bother my mother.

Once I heard a passing neighbor call out to my mother, "Is that another new dress?"

Mother answered, "It sure is!" Then she turned to me, smiled, and added quietly, "It's new to me." Because she realized I knew she had bought it used from a resale shop and then spent one entire evening remaking it.

. . .

Families aren't the only mentors who can help us gain insight. Mrs. Miller, my high school English teacher, helped me think about the choices I was making, particularly the kinds of people I was spending time with.

I learned from just being around and observing the adults I admired: Mr. Jaeck, Mr. McCotter, and Mr. Doakes. I watched their actions and how they thought and made decisions.

But you can also go directly to a mentor when you need a different perspective. Ask questions such as:

- What do you think about the experience and/or challenge going on in my life right now?

- Has anything like that ever happened to you?

- How have you seen other people handle similar situations?

- Do you have any questions you think I should be considering or asking myself as a means of thinking this through?

What a flow of information and eventual insight could come from such an approach if you connect with someone whose maturity and judgment you've come to respect, someone trust-worthy. If the person you approach knows you well already and sees your sincerity, chances are they will feel honored and do their best to give you a thoughtful response.

That doesn't mean every response will be thoughtful, help-ful, or particularly insightful—which is why you should prob-ably talk to more than one person. The combined observations and experiences of a few people could trigger some insight. Sometimes consensus can be a good thing.

One caution: Beware of looking for helpful insights from any random sampling of people or from your social network, which can be composed of much larger numbers of "friends" than I ever had to contend with. No matter how strong and independent-minded you might be, there is enormous pressure in any group to conform, to buy into what everybody else thinks is cool, and not to say or do anything to rock the boat or lose your own social status. That's one reason I think we should spell it P.E.E.R.S., because it stands for People Encouraging Errors, Rudeness, and Stupidity. It requires courage and conviction to step outside the circle. And I would add that peer pressure and its accompanying groupthink are the polar opposite of insight—because it means somebody else has already done your thinking for you.

. . .

Many of the most important insights I've had came as a result of reading. The day I identified obsidian in Mr. Jaeck's class, I realized I had known the answer to the question simply and only because I had been reading. Another related insight soon followed when I realized if I could learn about obsidian, I could learn the same way about social studies, geog-raphy, math, and science—everything I needed to learn to be the person I wanted to be. I knew then that reading would be my ticket out of ignorance and out of poverty; reading gave me a new measure of control over my future.

When you think about it, the connection between reading and insight makes sense. The starting point from which insights arise is knowledge acquired from observation and life experience. Books comprise stories that allow us to observe the lives and experiences of others. Other books merely convey knowledge. Books are really just another way for us to encounter different "mentors"—the authors—who pass on to us the very sort of empirical data required for insight: how other people think; how things work; cause and effect; and so much more.

A great number of books I enjoyed most during my teen and young adult years were biographies and autobiographies of people who experienced and overcame great hardship and obstacles to achieve impressive things in life. From so many of those true stories, I realized that life held a lot more possibilities. My own choices could direct and determine my future. Recognizing those truths gave me a sense of power over my own life, a freedom from feeling tossed about by events and circumstances I couldn't control.

For me, reading the Bible started during our family's weekly tradition of welcoming the Sabbath. Remember, Mother couldn't read, so Curtis and I would do the reading; then she would comment on it.

I clearly remember the story of David and Goliath and drawing the correlation that underdogs, like David, are not always as disadvantaged as they seem. The application I made of that insight was that we often have more resources than we think we do and that knowing and praying to God could be one of those.

I ask God to give me insight on a regular basis, especially before reading my daily chapter of wisdom from the Book of Proverbs. I believe it's God's Word, knowledge and truth he has given us all. And I usually find something that applies to my life for that day. My regular practice of looking for and finding practical advice for living began the day of the stabbing incident when I was fourteen. In my horror over having come so close to killing my friend, I believe God used the seriousness of that incident to give me a sobering insight: my out-of-control anger, which I'd always tried to shrug off, could and would derail my dreams and destroy my future if I didn't make some changes.

That terrified me. But what scared me even more was the helplessness and fear that came from knowing I didn't have a clue how to change. That's when I called out in desperation to God, and he prompted me to get my Bible, which I "just happened" to open, and begin reading Proverbs, where there were so many verses warning about anger.

What had been the worst day was transformed into one of the most wonderful turning points because of the insight and direction God gave me when I prayed.

I want to make certain I'm not leaving you imagining that insight is some mysterious, magical occurrence that suddenly pops out and provides you answers for every, or any, problem. Or is it some gift you are given with no assembly required.

We talked in Chapter 14 about time and its role and relationship to talent as well as to the practice and the goal of thinking big. And we'll touch on how learning and initiative tie into that philosophy. Here it's important to understand that these factors are all necessary to nurture and develop insight—because insight results from and is a part of a process. The more you acquire knowledge, the better your odds of gaining insight. But even a lot of raw knowledge won't ever equate to insight unless you reflect upon it enough to ask and answer as many questions as you can about it.

For example, if I'm reflecting on my own observations and experience with a certain person or problem, I will honestly ask myself questions such as these: What is happening here? How did I find myself in this situation? Have I faced similar predicaments before? How was that instance different from this one? Where is it the same? Based on past experience, what can I expect to happen if I do this, and what do I think might happen if I take this other approach? Why did this happen? What can I take from this?

Insight often comes after carefully examining the knowledge you have and using discernment to differentiate between the pieces you have assimilated. Wise people make those kinds of analyses. Foolish people seldom do so—which is why they keep doing the same ineffective things over and over. Sadly, it seems there's never a shortage of fools in our world. So I think it's safe to say that much of the world needs a lot more insight. It's not the same thing as wisdom, but it's part of the path and process that leads to it.

CHAPTER 17

Nice

When I was twelve years old, a group of kids started what we called the Helping Hands Club in our neighborhood. We'd walk around looking for someone who needed help. If we saw someone digging weeds, we'd say, "We'd like to help you." Then we'd pitch in and dig alongside them. The adults really appreciated that.

We didn't charge for our work, but we usually got paid. Sometimes a quarter or fifty cents, or even as much as a dollar. Or, sometimes, weeks later we'd see someone we'd helped; that person would recognize us and offer candy or ice cream. They became friendly to the members of our club because they liked us.

That's how I and other kids in our neighborhood learned that if we were nice, we would be rewarded. Even with a dollar being worth a lot more in those days, the greatest reward was never monetary; it was the positive relationships we developed with our neighbors and the personal satisfaction of doing something positive, unselfish, and nice for someone else.

That lesson stuck with me. And as I tried to apply it in other areas, I found it such a powerful factor in my personal and professional life. So when I began to share my thoughts and advice on success with audiences young and old, I quickly decided nice had to be the "N" in my THINK BIG philosophy.

I define nice with a list of synonyms: thoughtful, gentle, considerate, caring, pleasant, polite, agreeable, congenial, helpful—all of which add up to something close to, but not quite equal to, the idea I hope to convey when I say "nice." Being nice means the following.

- Don't talk about people behind their backs.
- Don't put people down in front of their backs.
- If you see somebody struggling with something, help him or her with it.
- Put yourself in the other person's place before you criticize.
- If the elevator door is open and only one space is left, let someone else get on.
- When driving, if someone puts a blinker on, slow down and let him or her in.
- Speak to people. Say "Good morning" or "Hello" to those you meet in the school hallway.
- Greet people by name whenever you can.

When I put niceness in those terms, most people understand exactly what I am talking about.

I remember speaking at a conference in the San Francisco Bay area years ago. I told my listeners, "If you're not a nice person, I challenge you to try it for one week ... It's ten minutes before ten on Friday morning. Until 9:50 next Friday morning, be nice to everybody—smile and greet the people you encounter ... Once they get over their initial shock, most people will be happy to greet you in return. You'll find that being nice is often contagious."

About 5:30 that evening, I was walking through the hotel lobby when I heard a woman calling, "Oh, Dr. Carson! Dr. Carson!" I stopped and turned to find a fashionably dressed woman in her fifties zigzagging her way toward me.

She introduced herself and said, "I want to tell you how much I appreciated your talk this morning. You actually made me cry."

She told me she had taken my challenge to be nice to everyone she met. "I already feel like a new person." She not only felt good about herself, but she had also been amazed by people's reactions. Her day had become an adventure as she wondered, *Whom can I be nice to next?* As we parted company, she said, "I think you've changed my life."

Over the years, I have discovered several reasons for being nice:

First, you get more done by being nice—whether you are merely trying to communicate or you are actually trying to accomplish a major task. Two brief scenarios:

Not long ago, Candy and I made a trip to France. Before we left we brushed up on the language, which we hadn't spoken since our college French courses. Neither of us was fluent, but we thought it would be nice to make an effort to converse with our hosts in their native tongue. Though we did it to be polite, we quickly discovered the greater benefit.

Most of the French people we met spoke much better English than our French, so invariably, after listening to our feeble attempts to converse in their language, they gladly began to use ours. We were then able to have much more helpful and interesting conversations than would have been possible had we simply expected them to communicate in our language from the start. They clearly appreciated our efforts, and our goodwill was more than repaid in kind.

Being nice also pays off professionally. I am well aware that across the field of medicine and in most hospitals, surgeons often have a reputation for being hard to get along with—and neurosurgeons are often the prickliest, most unpleasant of all. Some colleagues might excuse this by saying our job is so demanding and exacting because our decisions and actions mean the difference between life and death for our patients. Therefore, we need and expect a constant standard of excellence and immediate, maximum professional effort from everyone working with us. We have to be so focused on what we're thinking, seeing, and doing that there's a natural tendency for us to be snippy, impatient, demanding, critical, and otherwise oblivious to the feelings and perspectives of those around us. If we're not careful we can take out our own tension, tiredness, frustration, our fear of failure, and our sense of desperation on those working with us. We may trample all over the feelings of the very people we have to count on every day.

Yet I could not do my job as a surgeon without the assistance and expertise of many other people—not only in the OR, but also in recovery, the wards, labs, other hospital departments, my office, and everywhere my patients (and their medical records) go. I quickly learned that if I make a consistent, daily effort to be nice to the folks I encounter and work with—whether that person is a fellow surgeon or a filing clerk in radiology tracking down a lost X-ray—they tend to be nicer back to me. If I've made a habit of greeting them by name when I can, thanking them for their help, commending them for quick and efficient work, and knowing them well enough to ask about their kids' most recent sports achievements or their spouse's current job, those people cooperate faster and try harder to accomplish anything I ask of them.

I'm not talking about getting what I want by being manipulative. I'm merely saying, be nice. The positive attitudes that usually result help improve others' performance and mine as well.

Second, being nice feels good. The lady who caught me in that San Francisco hotel lobby discovered this in just a few hours. My friends and I discovered it with our Helping Hands Club. I've experienced it in my professional and personal relationships. Being nice is simply a better way to live—and its own reward.

Everyone is worth it. Being nice is a simple, practical, concrete way to acknowledge the uniqueness God created in every individual and to show each person we encounter the respect and dignity he or she deserves. It demonstrates a spirit of democracy that says we think other people matter.

We like to think of America as a classless society, but if we are honest, we have to admit that we are divided into many categories—ethnically, racially, economically, educationally, socially, geographically. Being nice to everyone is the simplest way I know to lower the artificial barriers human beings have erected.

During college, I remember people who were loners. Everyone else would be slapping each other's backs and having a good time, while the loners would be sitting off in a corner—eating lunch by themselves. Perhaps I empathized because I was something of an introvert myself. Often I would take a seat close to a loner—not directly next to them but sort of catty-corner. Then I'd try to start a conversation to see if they were looking for somebody to talk to. Most of the time, they were. I was actually able to develop a number of friendly relationships like that. And some of those loners turned out to be really great people. They just needed a little prodding to open up. One of them turned out to be very helpful to me with calculus, and our relationship became a two-way street.

Being nice is much easier in the long run.

We have all heard that smiling requires less energy and fewer muscles than frowning. The same economy-of-effort idea holds true in most human interactions. Reduced tension and increased goodwill add up to greater efficiency. You seldom make enemies by being nice, and life without enemies is always easier. Doctors whose patients think they are nice do not get sued as often—and that certainly made my professional life a lot easier.

You never lose by being nice. It seldom costs anything, except a little time, thought, and energy. Sure, you occasionally run into people who will take advantage of your kindness; they might even consider niceness to be a weakness. But in the end, niceness wins out.

. . .

We may all agree that being nice is a good thing. But some of us struggle with the how. If you have gotten out of the habit, or you want to be more consistently nice, try the following steps.

1. TAKE YOURSELF OUT OF THE EQUATION. Whatever the setting—home, school, church, extracurricular activities—one of the keys to being perceived as a nice person is to take your ego out of the picture. This is crucial whether you're in a conflict, casual exchange, or deeply personal relationship.

2. TRY TO LOOK AT THE OTHER PERSON'S POINT OF VIEW. This helps some people accomplish step one. Either way, these two strategies seem to work best in tandem. We can usually gain a better perspective if we look at life not just from our own vantage point but from the other person's position as well. When we consider their feelings, ideas, and motives, we'll find it much easier to be nice.

3. JUST LISTEN. Listening automatically takes you out of the center of the equation and helps you see the other person's viewpoint. When you listen, you validate a person's worth and recognize the respect and dignity they deserve.

I learned early in my medical career that the single most valuable thing I could do for patients is to listen. Many of them were too young to tell me anything, so I listened to their parents. I cannot count the number of times a patient's mother has told me something important about her child, some medically significant clue I would not have learned from any examination or test, a clue that enabled me to successfully diagnose and treat the problem.

4. PUT ASIDE PERSONAL PREFERENCE. People who cannot be nice remind me of children in the back of a car, bickering over who gets to sit by the window. Fortunately, most children develop a more mature perspective as they grow older and backseat squabbles diminish. And yet some never want to give up the window, putting their own preferences aside. I can think of one instance in which I have had to learn to do this.

For most of my adult life, I have been a vegetarian. But out of consideration — in other words, to be nice — I have learned to eat chicken or turkey in situations where I cannot gracefully manage to have a vegetarian meal. My wife and I still laugh about the time we were invited to a small dinner party at the home of friends who had forgotten we were vegetarians. The main course that night happened to be pork chops with pineapple topping. I have never eaten pork, and among so few guests, I knew my avoidance of the entree would not go unnoticed. So I served myself rice and vegetables then scooped some of the pineapple onto my rice, hoping it might look as though a pork chop were lurking underneath there somewhere. I also hoped the hostess would not notice.

No such luck. Unfortunately, the flavor of the pork had soaked into the pineapple and made me so nauseated that I could not eat. When our hostess realized the problem, she was embarrassed anyway. She too tried to be nice by not calling attention to me, but she appreciated the fact that at least I had tried to avoid hurting her feelings. So in that case, merely the attempt to be nice made a difference.

5. LEARN TO LOVE PEOPLE. If you really love people, being nice to them is almost second nature. For me, this strategy is closely connected to my own personal faith. I believe what the Bible says in 1 John 4:19–21: "We love because he first loved us. Whoever

claims to love God yet hates a brother or sister is a liar. For whoever does not love their brother and sister, whom they have seen, cannot love God, whom they have not seen. And he has given us this command: Anyone who loves God must also love their brother and sister." If I say I love God, I have no choice but to show it by loving and being nice to other people.

6. DO UNTO OTHERS ... We can forget all five of these prior strategies if we just remember the best strategy of all: the Golden Rule, which Jesus gave his followers. He boils the entire "be nice" idea down to one simple sentence: "Do to others as you would have them do to you" (Luke 6:31). That is not only the simplest and best way to take yourself out of the equation, but it is also the most comprehensive plan for being nice.

Even though it is true that some people will take advantage of kindness and might even consider it a weakness, in the long run, kindness prevails. Yet being nice doesn't mean being a wimp or letting others hurt or take advantage of you. Being nice is a choice. It cannot be dictated by circumstances or forced on you against your will. It is a conscious decision, requiring determination, conviction, and strength of character.

In the case of the woman who falsely accused me of fathering her child, I chose to be forgiving and not pursue legal action. But there was another case recently where I decided I could not risk being so nice. A woman from New York whom I had never met evidently became infatuated with me. She wrote me countless letters and enclosed nude pictures of herself. When I did not respond, she began to make wild threats. Her letters became so irrational that my lawyer and a psychiatrist advised me to make arrangements for special security whenever I traveled to the New York City area.

I also decided the danger warranted legal action. So the state's attorneys from Maryland and New York had to get involved until this woman realized the gravity of the situation and quit harassing me.

• • •

I concluded long ago that if two people always agree on every-thing, then one of those people is probably not needed. So I neither expect nor want the people I work or live with to always agree with me. But we can be nice to each other when express-ing an opinion the other person does not want to hear. This reminds me of a conversation I had with a final-year medical school student.

He quickly told me his story. He admitted to feeling a kinship with me; despite growing up in poverty, he too had set himself the lofty goal of becoming a doctor. Throughout his academic career, this young man did well in the classroom but always struggled with standardized tests. That pattern held true in medical school as well.

He explained to me how he'd completed all his course work, passed his classes with flying colors, but after four years of hard work, he had done so poorly on his comprehensive exams that the school had ruled him ineligible to graduate that year. He was advised that before he could receive his degree he would have to retake three courses and sufficiently demonstrate his mastery of that material. He had just learned the ruling and was embar-rassed, frustrated, angry, and devastated. More than anything, he was afraid his lifelong dream would be lost. He didn't know what he should do. Ultimately, he believed this administrative decision was a form of discrimination. At the urging of some of his friends and family, he was considering legal action. But he wondered what I thought he should do.

I empathized with this young man's frustrations, fears, and concerns. But I quickly realized he wanted my approval to validate his feelings, to justify his angry response, and as an endorsement to sue. Instead, I pointed out that no one had said he would not be able to graduate. Neither had they said they thought he was incapable of becoming a doctor. The fact that he failed to make the required grade on his comps was more indicative of his own lifelong problem with standardized testing than it was evidence of any discrimination. Yet no one had closed the door to his dream; they had actually found a way to leave the door open. All that his advisor had said was that he would be required to take three additional courses to prove that he knew what he needed to know to be a good doctor. His disappointment and embarrassment were understandable, but I told him what I thought would be his simplest and best course of action: "I would advise you to retake the courses."

My response was not what that young student wanted to hear. Yet the moment I said it, the emotion and tension drained out of that room like air out of a balloon. He did not argue. After thanking me for my advice, we parted company. I later learned that he had followed my advice, took the courses, passed the test to everyone's satisfaction, and is a doctor today.

And whenever I think about that young man, I am reminded that being nice does not mean we always have to agree.

Niceness and honesty are not incompatible. In fact, truthfulness plus kindness equals tact. And tact is wonderfully illustrated by my friend and longtime colleague Dr. Levi Watkins, a noted cardiovascular surgeon. As the first black chief resident in cardiac surgery at Johns Hopkins, Levi's numerous professional accomplishments include the first successful implantation of the automatic cardiac defibrillator (a device that can prevent fatal cardiac arrhythmias). Not only is he recognized throughout the world for his professional contribution to medical science that has saved millions of lives, but Levi was also known throughout our Johns Hopkins community as being an exceedingly nice man. His tenderhearted, caring nature brought all kinds of people with all kinds of personal problems to his office for advice. Yet Levi was known as much for his candor as for his kindness. Not long ago a resident who had a serious personality conflict with some of the attending physicians came to Levi to complain and seek his support in rectifying the situation. Levi checked into the situation and confirmed that the problem was indeed a personality conflict. Instead of trying to resolve the conflict, Levi suggested that the resident's best course of action would be to transfer to another hospital. He did so and did well in the new program.

Levi does not waste time hiding his feelings or opinions. He simply tells it like it is and doesn't compromise his standards. That is why his counsel is so widely valued.

Our best model for not compromising our standards is also our best model in every area of life: Jesus. He is not only the author of the ultimate standard of niceness—the Golden Rule— but he also taught and lived by higher standards than anyone else in history. Everything we know about Jesus Christ indicates he was certainly a nice person.

But that does not mean he excused sin or lowered his expectations of himself or others. He proved that it was possible to be loving, thoughtful, gentle, considerate, and caring, yet still hold to and live by an unwavering belief that wrong is wrong and right is always right.

Before we leave this subject, I'd like to address an area of our modern culture where a lot of people compromise their standards and forget to be nice at all. I'm talking about the Internet and social media.

Most of us have so many virtual friends and acquaintances we connect with online—using whatever the hottest new apps and sites are this year, this month, this week—that it becomes all too easy to forget that behind every one of those usernames, Twitter handles, hash tags, and avatars is an actual human being with real feelings. So many of those participating in the pop culture trend of trolling the Internet to pick virtual fights and to gang up on others who stand—who have different ideas, different cultures, different standards, different politics, different faiths—seem to have forgotten their basic manners, social skills, morals, and (sometimes) even their humanity. If you wouldn't join in a mugging you saw taking place on a street, if you wouldn't physically attack or verbally abuse and cruelly insult an acquaintance in your school, why would you ever ridicule or hurl vicious and hurtful words at a person online?

Virtual violence can cause real pain and suffering in the real world. Before you shrug that off, look up and read some of the well-publicized and tragic cases where young people (and some not-so-young people) have committed suicide in the wake of being cruelly attacked, vilified, ridiculed, embarrassed, or exposed on the Internet where anyone with access to a computer can witness their humiliation. That so many think such behavior is entertaining is a sad commentary on our culture. And it's the extreme and total opposite of nice.

Be nice. It's such an elementary concept. Yet I probably get as much reaction to this one as any other topic I speak about—which underscores the importance of this seemingly simple, very practical, and exceedingly valuable idea.

CHAPTER 18

Knowledge

Starting that day in fifth grade when my knowledge about obsidian impressed Mr. Jaeck, my classmates, and myself, I was suddenly persuaded that knowledge was the key to prove I was not the dummy everyone thought I was.

Over the years, I gained as much knowledge as I could. My forensics competitions during high school enabled me to become a more confident and effective oral communicator in front of all types of audiences. That knowledge provided me an advantage in my profession whether I was sharing my opinion in meetings with colleagues, lecturing in medical school classes, or briefing the press after some news-making surgery. That knowledge also equipped me for a gratifying second career as a public speaker over the last twenty-five years, and more recently as a contributor and commentator on a major television news network.

As an unpaid lab assistant to my tenth-grade biology teacher, I so impressed a college professor that he gave me a paid job at Wayne State University before I ever graduated from high school. I added to that knowledge base at every stage of my education and professions, so my skill level and familiarity with lab procedures gave me a leg up on my classmates and many colleagues.

Remember how my knowledge of classical music so surprised and impressed my interviewer for the Johns Hopkins residency program that I edged out the other 124 very qualified applicants? Many times I have looked back over my life and remembered how high school friends would shake their heads and laugh at me for listening to "crazy old classical" stuff while they would be grooving to Motown. Not that I didn't enjoy the Top Forty tunes of the day, but the knowledge my friends considered "useless," "silly," and frankly "kinda strange" proved instrumental (music pun intended) at a life-changing point. This scenario is probably the best illustration of what I've told thousands of young people around the world: There is no such thing as useless knowledge, because you never know what little bit of information will open certain doors for you.

Knowledge—the "K" in THINK BIG—has the power to make you into a more valuable person. Yes, I own a big house and drive nice cars. I have many of the things that money can buy. But are my house and my cars important? Of course not. If somebody comes along and takes it all away, it's no big deal. I can get it all back using what's inside my head.

In Proverbs and Ecclesiastes, King Solomon talked about gold, silver, and rubies being nice but that knowledge, wisdom, and understanding should be treasured far above all those things (Proverbs 16:16). Plus, with knowledge, wisdom, and understanding, you can get all the gold, silver, and rubies you need—yet what you come to understand is that riches aren't really all that important.

. . .

Back in fifth grade, I tried to act nonchalant, but I detested the other kids' ridicule. I greatly admired—and yes, even envied—those kids who raised their hands and knew the answers. I often wondered, *How is that possible? They're the same age I am, in the same grade. How can they possibly know all this stuff I don't know?*

Then my mother made us read those books. And soon after that, when a teacher asked a question, and another student answered, I would think, *I knew that answer, too.*

Prior to that I'd felt like a hapless old prospector, searching and digging everywhere for gold but without a shovel. Then someone gave me one. The books I was reading became my shovel. And the gold I was suddenly discovering, digging up, and stashing away? That was knowledge.

Once I realized I'd struck a virtual mother lode, I became very motivated to "shovel" all the more. And the growing treasure of knowledge I gained accelerated my progression from the bottom to the top of the class.

One day another student in my class began waxing eloquently about some current event. I wondered how he had so much knowledge about the subject and found out he liked to watch the evening news. So I started watching the news, something that I continue to this day.

Over the years, I've encountered many people who seemed to be amazed that a doctor could be knowledgeable about some changing policy of the Russian government and its impact on Europe, the historic differences between Shiite and Sunni Muslims, or which countries suffered the worst economic devastation from the latest typhoon to ravage Southeast Asia. What I considered basic facts, accessible to anyone in America with a television set, has over the years made me somehow more credible in the eyes of other people. I suspect that explains, in part, how I became a television news commentator after I retired as a surgeon. And why a lot of people, since my retirement, are encouraging me to consider running for president of the United States. Talk about thinking big!

...

As I've thought about knowledge during the course of my life, I've tried to inspire and challenge others to grasp its value. So I've identified a variety of practical ways people can acquire useful and life-changing knowledge.

Often young people, and even some adults, hear my story

and say, "But I'm not much of a reader," "Reading is hard for me. I read so slowly," or "I don't retain what I read." My first response is: reading is a learned skill. So as with any learned skill, you can improve it with practice. The more you do it, the better you'll be at it. Motivate yourself and retain what you read by reading books on subjects that already interest you—as I did with animals. And if you force yourself to read fast, there's a good chance you will not only become a faster reader, but you'll also be more attentive to what you read. Your brain can get bored when you read slowly—speedier reading can imply a sense of movement in your mind.

Let me add that there are some people whose struggle, and lack of ability to read is due to physiological or neurological issues in the brain itself, including learning disabilities such as dyslexia. Yet I find it fascinating that so many dyslexic people have been able to face that challenge and lead normal, even successful, lives.

Indeed, Malcolm Gladwell, in his bestselling book *David and Goliath: Underdogs, Misfits, and the Art of Battling Giants,* offers an impressive list of dyslexic entrepreneurs and tells the stories of two highly successful dyslexics, David Boies (one of the most famous trial lawyers in the world) and Gary Cohn (president of the Wall Street financial powerhouse Goldman Sachs.)

Both men acknowledge their lifelong struggles with reading, yet they are quick to acknowledge the possibility they might never have achieved what they have had they not been severely dyslexic. While Boies admitted an average ability to read would have made life simpler and easier, having to learn mostly by listening and asking questions forced him to boil down issues and arguments to their basics. He also needed to speak in simple words using short sentences, or he would get tongue-tied. The knowledge and skill he acquired doing that made David Boies an especially clear and effective communicator when addressing judges or juries.

Gary Cohn admits to being a troubled student who pretended not to care, goofed off, and acted up in school in order to hide how much it bothered him that he didn't measure up to his classmates. (I can relate to that.) He got expelled the first time in fourth grade and kicked out of school after that, during what he calls "the ugly years." When he finally graduated from high school, his mother couldn't hide her relief and joy. Gary says never before or since has he ever seen anyone cry more than his mom did on that graduation day.

He surprised his parents when he got into college. But once he'd 1) figured out his strengths were in numbers not words and language; 2) matured enough not to get kicked out of classes; and 3) realized he needed to work harder than his classmates to learn enough to pass, Gary Cohn earned his college degree at the age of twenty-two. After a brief career selling aluminum window frames and siding, he met a commodities trader in New York City and talked the man into giving him a job by pretending to understand options trading.

And the rest is Wall Street legend. Cohn told Gladwell, "My upbringing allowed me to be comfortable with failure," a trait he believes is shared with "a lot of dyslexic people I know ... by the time we got out of college, our ability to deal with failure was very highly developed ... It doesn't faze us."[3] Cohn also observed that as dyslexics are people who can't read well, they tend to build a good sense of listening.[4] That attitude and understanding how to cope with failure would be critical knowledge for any leader in the often-risky, high-stakes world of high finance.

---

3. Malcolm Gladwell, *David & Goliath,* (New York: Little, Brown & Co., 2013).

4. CBS News, *Sixty Minutes,* "Malcolm Gladwell: The Power of the Underdog," Nov. 24, 2013. www.cbsnews.com/videos/malcolm-gladwell-the-power-of-the-underdog/.

I share these examples as reminders that knowledge can be gained in more than one way. But I also see people like David Boies and Gary Cohn as encouraging proof that the human brain is amazingly adaptable. It can, in many cases, work around physiological/neurological glitches in its own circuitry to acquire knowledge in surprisingly original and advantageous ways.

I've experienced that in my own life because I am color-blind—which presented a challenge for me in my histology and pathology courses during med school. We were expected to distinguish red cells from pink or blue cells under a microscope in order to note and diagnose varying degrees of inflammation. The fact that I couldn't differentiate between cells the easy way meant I concentrated my attention on other differences—size, shape, direction, and subtler variations. That profoundly impacted my observations and knowledge of those cells. Later, when we began to look at mutations in cells, I could recognize them more quickly because I was already used to noting more characteristics than color.

Do I wish I didn't have to depend on my wife to make sure my ties don't clash with my shirts or my suits? Of course. But whenever Candy teases me about being color-challenged, I try to persuade her that "color blindness is a sign of superior intelligence." She laughingly says, "You think whatever you have is a sign of superior intelligence." "That's right!" I tell her in a joking tone that implies, don't you forget it. While I don't truly believe that claim, I am convinced the knowledge I gained in compensating for my color blindness made me stronger as a doctor.

Want more evidence? Consider how the brain of a blind person can still access written language by reading braille through the sense of touch in the fingertips. Or how the hearing impaired can acquire language not only through reading words off a page, but also by interpreting and translating signs from visual images their optical nerves transmit to the brain.

Certainly we have reason to be amazed by all Helen Keller learned and accomplished without the benefit of hearing or sight. Her life represented a great triumph of the human spirit. But I believe her story is just as much a tribute to the potential, capacity, and adaptability of the human brain.

Remember my first hemispherectomy patient, Maranda Francisco? We wondered if she would ever learn to speak, see, or walk again when we removed the entire left side of the brain, the side that controls human speech and the motor controls for the entire right side of the body.

We didn't have to wait long for our answers. On the gurney during her transfer from the Operating Room (OR) to recovery, Maranda opened her eyes, saw her parents, told them she loved them, and began squirming around enough to indicate neither of her right extremities was paralyzed. The right side of her brain had immediately begun to adapt, compensate, and take over the essential roles of the missing left hemisphere. Maranda didn't merely survive; she thrived. As did many hemispherectomy patients to follow, who recovered, attained an education, and went on to live normal lives, raising families of their own and in quite a few cases even graduating from college—all with only half a brain.

Some people reading my hemispherectomy stories might consider them evidence of the oft-repeated claim that human beings only use 10 percent of their brains. Actually, unless we have some degree of physical/neurological brain damage, we all use all of our brains—but little of our potential. That's where the 10 percent idea comes in, and that's probably a very generous estimation.

I say that because the electrical circuitry in the average human brain contains billions of neurons and hundreds of billions of interconnections, capable of processing two million bytes of information per second. Your brain can remember everything you have ever seen or heard. Every part of this magnificently interwoven system participates in some of all we do throughout our lives. God gave each of us brains with such amazing capacity and almost infinite potential.

I've talked quite a bit here about how you can acquire knowledge. But what are some other common "shovels" to use to find knowledge? And where are the most promising places to be digging?

To start, just living through whatever life throws at you provides a rich source of knowledge. Through simple observation as a tool (shovel), you can pick up knowledge. But you have to pay attention, actively looking for the knowledge you encounter. Only then will you recognize it, assay its value, take note, and consciously file it securely away in your brain for later use.

The life experience of failure is a surprisingly rich source of knowledge.

A personal example: My second experience with craniopagus Siamese twins in South Africa in 1994 certainly seemed to be a failure, from a human perspective. All that effort! Months of meticulous preparations. The expense of acquiring all that equipment. And the hopes, prayers, and work of more than sixty doctors, nurses, and technicians. Still, both girls died.

We had no way of knowing, before the surgery, that the Makwaeba sisters had been entirely symbiotic. We only knew that if we didn't operate, the girls would die. But, of course, we learned that even with the surgery, the two of them could not have lived.

Having a medical explanation for the girls' death didn't make me feel any less devastated by my sense of failure. None of it made sense—until almost three years later when the same South African neurosurgeon called to tell me about yet another craniopagus twin case and to ask if I'd come back to lead the same surgical team again. This time, in large part because of what I'd learned, what he'd learned, and the knowledge his surgical and hospital teams had gained during that previous "failure" experience, Zambian twin brothers Luka and Joseph Banda were successfully separated. They not only survived the surgery, but they also made remarkably full recoveries.

The vast majority of the greatest medical discoveries and advancements throughout history have been achieved, in part, after previous failures in diagnoses, treatment, or procedures. The same can be said about most, if not all, the historic progress in any of the sciences. Thomas Edison supposedly said he discovered how an electric lightbulb worked only after learning how ten thousand didn't work. How many times did the Wright brothers fail before they acquired enough knowledge to finally fly at Kitty Hawk?

So I recommend the benefits of embracing new opportunities and experiences of your own choosing. Some first steps might be as simple as sampling some ethnic food you've never tried before, or finding a friend with an unusual but intriguing hobby you know little about and asking him or her to explain the basics. Making a habit of experiencing new things in little ways can help you think bigger so you embrace more significant opportunities when they present themselves.

One such opportunity I touched on earlier was the decision Candy and I made to go to Australia so I could do another year of surgical training under one of the top neurosurgeons. Australia held many uncertainties. So we asked family, friends, and colleagues for their thoughts and advice. Several folks mentioned that Australia didn't have a great history when it came to welcoming and accepting black people. We heard what was said, then we did some more research. (Always a good idea.) We learned there had indeed been some regrettable racial issues in the past, but that laws had been changed years before. The people we talked to who lived in Australia, and those who'd visited most recently, assured us we would be graciously welcomed and accepted. They were right.

What we learned from our cross-cultural experience enriched our lives. And the breadth of skills and the depth of knowledge I gained during that year was perhaps the biggest factor in me even being considered, and ultimately chosen, to be head of pediatric neurosurgery at Johns Hopkins at the unprecedented age of thirty-three.

A new experience can serve as an effective shovel for accessing a world of new knowledge—if you're willing to take the risk.

Other reliable sources of knowledge have been mentors who influenced me at various stages of my life. Some made the first move by showing an interest in me. Others I've chosen on my own because I believed I could benefit from knowing what they knew. If you can persuade those you are genuinely interested in knowing to teach you, you'll be surprised how many of those folks will be willing to impart as much as you can absorb.

Thinking big is a lot easier when those who went before you are willing to give you a leg up and let you stand on their shoulders. But knowledge by itself is never enough—even if it is from the world's purest and most reliable source—because there is a world of difference between knowledge and wisdom.

To be sure, knowledge is power. Wisdom is what's necessary to harness and direct it. Wisdom is what it takes to know what to do with our knowledge. Thinking big requires both.

CHAPTER 19

Books

Books did more than change the student I was; they changed the person I was. Books—the "B" in THINK BIG—transported me to another world, beyond poverty, where I experienced adventures in my imagination that no boy from the streets of Detroit could ever dream up. Reading didn't merely expand my horizons; it exploded my world so quickly and completely that my life was never the same. I soon felt as if I could never get enough of this amazing new feeling of excitement and freedom.

The first autobiography I ever read was *Up from Slavery* by Booker T. Washington. Born a slave, he risked severe punishment by learning to read as a boy. Yet through reading, he educated himself to the point that he became a friend and advisor to presidents. Was it possible that what worked for Booker T. Washington might have the same kind of impact on my life?

A second hero of mine, born into slavery on a plantation in Maryland—where I've lived most of my adult life—shared a story much like Booker T's. Early in his life, the plantation owners selected Frederick Douglass to live in their house. His mother, who wasn't a constant presence in his life, died when he was seven or so. One of the plantation owners was possibly his father; he never knew for certain.

Frederick eventually became a servant in the Baltimore home of a man named Hugh Auld. Mrs. Auld, who had no prior experience with slaves, began to teach him the alphabet. When her husband learned what she was doing, he angrily ordered an immediate end to the lessons, telling her that educating slaves ruins them by making them discontented and therefore unmanageable. Frederick overheard his master's tirade: a sudden revelation of the strategy white men used to enslave blacks. Frederick knew then the first thing he needed to do if ever he was to win his freedom. He sought out the company of white children and others in the neighborhood, from whom he continued to learn. Whenever the Aulds were away, Frederick would practice his letters by carefully writing out words in some of the old lesson books the Aulds' son had left around the house. Soon he was reading whenever and wherever he could without being discovered.[5]

One of the earliest books he read had a chapter that was written in the form of a discussion, a master arguing the philosophical and moral case for slavery, with his slave then addressing and debating each of his owner's arguments. That book planted a seed of abolitionist conviction that took root and grew strong and fast in the heart and mind of young Frederick. Eventually, around the age of twenty, he escaped and fled north to live in Massachusetts among a community of freed men. There he became an accomplished orator, writer, and one of the most effective and famous antislavery voices in America in the years before the Civil War.

Frederick Douglass informed the world of what he learned as a boy—that a knowledgeable man does not make a good slave. He explained, "Once you learn to read, you will be forever free."[6]

Once I discovered books, I knew just how he felt.

Frederick Douglass, Booker T. Washington, and countless others like them grasped an important truth that literally could, and did, set them free. The reason it was illegal for slaves to read

---

5. Frederick Douglass, *Narrative of the Life of Frederick Douglass* (Dover Publications, 1995).

6. The Frederick Douglass Organization, 2014, http://frederickdouglassiv.org.

was because, like Mr. Auld, most slave owners knew that knowledge is power. They understood it is difficult, if not impossible, to hold in captivity anyone who is knowledgeable. Reading first freed the mind, the imagination, and the soul of literate slaves — and eventually brought the destruction of the long, shameful institution of slavery in America.

Let me give you a couple other contemporary examples.

Books played a powerful role in the life of my friend Walter Anderson. Walter grew up in a four-room railroad flat with an abusive, alcoholic father. "I lived with fear every day, nearly every minute, of my childhood," he remembers. "Often my father would beat me for things I might do, not for things I had done. I felt safer on the street corner than in my own home."

His mother tried to shield him from his father's abuse. And she encouraged him to read, even though his father would beat him if he caught Walter with a book. She believed, much like my mother did, that if Walter could read, he could find his way out of their life.

The public library became a secret sanctuary where Walter regularly escaped his father's abuse and the cruel ridicule of classmates who would laugh at the holes in his ragged clothes. "I read myself out of poverty long before I worked myself out of poverty," he says. "By reading, I could go anywhere, I could be anybody, and I could do anything. I could imagine myself out of a slum."[7]

Six days after his seventeenth birthday, he found another way out. He joined the Marines. "I was able to develop self-respect, self-esteem, and a belief in noble motives and noble purposes. I learned about honor and dignity." In 1965, just months before he was to complete his active duty, Walter volunteered for Vietnam.[8]

---

7. http://www.horatioalger.org/members_info.cfm?memberid=and94
8. Ibid.

When he returned home from overseas, Walter first took a job as a laboratory assistant, then as a sales trainee. But what he wanted to do more than anything else was to write. "Ever since I was fourteen or fifteen years old, I had a tremendous need to express myself," he said.

Carrying the only thing he had ever had published—an emotional and articulate letter to the editor (titled "Just What Is Vietnam?") in his hometown paper, the *Mt. Vernon Daily Argus*—Walter walked into a newspaper office to plead for a job. After reading Walter's one-clipping portfolio, the editor of the *Reporter Dispatch* in White Plains, New York, hired him for ninety dollars a week.

While working as a reporter in White Plains, Walter enrolled in a community college and graduated two years later—first in his class of six hundred students. By that time he was night editor of his paper and had started his own action-line column, which was syndicated in seven other newspapers. Nearby Mercy College awarded him a full scholarship to continue his education. He graduated from there summa cum laude, once again class valedictorian.

After serving as editor and general manager of two daily newspapers, he moved to *Parade* magazine, the largest circulation Sunday magazine in the world, as managing editor. Then at the age of thirty-five, he was promoted to editor. From the time he took over the editorial reins of *Parade* in 1980, until he was inducted into the Horatio Alger Association of Distinguished Americans with me, circulation of his magazine had risen from 21 million copies in 129 Sunday newspapers to more than 37 million copies in 353 papers.

Walter discovered the value in reading and the power of words as a lonely boy searching for hope and escape. He then spent a lifetime wielding that power to provide information and value to millions.

My second example comes from another friend of mine, a successful retired lawyer and philanthropist by the name of William H. Gates, Sr. You've likely never heard of him, but you'd recognize his son, Microsoft founder Bill Gates.

I became acquainted with the elder Gates because we have served together for years on the corporate board of Costco Wholesale Corporation. I came to so respect his personal character and his years of impressive legal and business experience that Candy and I invited him to speak to the young (fourth- to eleventh-grade) scholarship recipients at the annual national awards banquet and gala for our Carson Scholars Fund.

In his brief but telling description of family life in the Gates' home, he proudly, and laughingly, recalled how young Bill, from the time he began to read, always had his nose in a book or a book in his hands. So much so that Mr. Gates had to establish the rule that there would be no open books at the supper table — at least while anyone was still eating.

Mr. Gates probably wasn't thrilled when Bill dropped out of college to pursue his fascination with computers and software. But even then Mr. Gates realized his son had already received and continued to acquire an education through his constant reading.

So my question for you is this: What role do you hope to play in this new era in which we are living today? In other words, how big are you willing to think? You get to make the decision. And the first step is to choose to read.

Whether you read pages of paper and ink or of light and electricity may not matter much at all because knowledge is absolutely essential to thinking big. And reading remains one of the simplest, best, and most basic means of accessing knowledge — and acquiring the freedom and power that comes with it.

. . .

In twenty-first century America, public education remains free. So the quality varies. Some teachers, some schools, and some school systems are better than others. But if you decide you cannot get an excellent education because your teacher is not effective, your school does not have high enough academic standards, or your school system is poorly funded, you are in danger of letting a victim mentality limit your future.

Ultimately, your education is up to you. Only you can decide how much you are going to empower yourself through learning and knowledge. How far you go is determined, largely, by how far you are willing to go. Any student who so desires can achieve a high-quality education, whoever or wherever they may be—as long as they can read.

Now let me say a few things about the Internet by acknowledging the fact that it can be a tremendous boon, or a serious barrier, to learning and the acquisition of knowledge. Of course, one positive aspect is anyone can immediately get information on pretty much anything. If you can spell your word, topic, quote, or question, you can find thousands of references in milliseconds and be reading up on the subject in less than a minute. The implications of such speedy access to information are tremendous. The problem, of course, is that going to the Internet can be much like listening to another person you just happen to meet on the street. You have no simple way of knowing whether they, their opinions, and their supposed "knowledge" are legitimate.

Sometimes they are. Your source might be an excellent and well-respected professor who knows exactly what he is writing about. But the next reference could link you to the website of a complete buffoon. So instant access is both the pro and the con of online information.

As a result, you must develop discernment about what you read online in order to sort out the good information from the bad, the true from the false. One of the best ways to do that is to multi-source everything you look up.

For example, when you type in *Battle of Monongahela* and hit return, Google will find you about one million results in 0.35 seconds. By doing a sampling of maybe ten of the most promising ones, you're going to get a pretty good idea about what the Battle of Monongahela was and its significance in history. You may acquire some authoritative and clearly trustworthy sources. But if you check only one of the links, you might hit a website where someone inexplicably posted one of his friend's brother's girlfriend's high-school American history term paper on the subject—which only received a C- because the teacher graded on a very liberal curve. Multi-source everything; even seemingly qualified sources might give you biased or a uniquely different slant on a topic that might not represent a consensus of the authorities.

Bear in mind, when you read a title from a reputable publishing house, they're going to be selective about what goes into a book with its name on it. The publisher has a reputation at stake. The same is often true of magazines and newspapers. Internet sites often have no such filter.

Ebooks may have similar filters to printed books—if published by a reputable publishing house. But there's a growing trend of self-published books, even among long-established authors, that are then sold online at Amazon, Barnes and Noble, and other online bookstores. This means you will need discernment as well as effort if you want to know the trustworthiness of any ebook author and her ideas.

Many developmental psychologists believe that overexposure to electronic media is contributing to what seems like an epidemic-like surge of attention deficit disorder (ADD), much of which I would prefer to diagnose and term pseudo ADD.

A quick example: I talked to a woman recently who informed me her son had ADD. I asked, "Is he able to watch a movie?"

She said, "Oh yeah, he can watch movies all day."

I asked, "Is he able to play video games?"

"Oh, my yes! He's an expert at video games. He can play for hours."

I told her, "He doesn't have ADD. He has pseudo ADD." He has no trouble at all paying attention to the kinds of things he has trained his mind to attend to.

Most of us are exposed to television, movies, video games, computers, tablets, smart phones, and the Internet on a daily basis. We need to ask ourselves: How many waking hours of my day do I spend interacting with (and paying attention to) electronic devices? Do I spend more time with my hundreds of Facebook friends each week than I do with the handful of my closest in-the-flesh friends? Do actual people, everyday thoughts, and real life seem less interesting, maybe even boring, compared to the ideas, activities, interactions, and people I encounter through electronic media?

If you honestly answer these questions in the affirmative, you may have an addiction or attention problem. Such problems limit the time you devote to reading and accumulating useful knowledge and retrain your brain, making it harder to think big.

In addition to weaning yourself off an excess of electronics, these simple strategies may help your attention to reading:

1. Try standing or pacing when you read; take a break every hour for ten to fifteen minutes. If you do that consistently, you start looking forward to that break and that gives you the energy to keep going.
2. Push yourself to read faster.
3. Read with dramatic expression to stimulate your imagination and keep awake.

I believe so strongly in the power and freedom to be discovered through books that our Carson Scholars foundation has begun providing Carson Reading Rooms in disadvantaged schools. My hope is that thousands of kids from backgrounds like mine will find what an incredible difference reading can make in their lives.

We've already created more than one hundred reading rooms around the country. Most are in Title I schools where many of the students come from homes with no books. Often such schools don't even have a library, so the kids have little or no opportunity to develop the joy of reading. The natural result is a high percentage of dropouts. Many social psychologists have reported what I learned from personal experience: when you learn to love reading early on, your chances of academic success skyrocket. And when you don't, just the opposite occurs.

Reading books does more than provide ready access to knowledge, it also 1) exercises and stretches the mind; 2) forces the mind to discriminate (in other words, to begin to think); and 3) pushes readers to use their imaginations and encourages creativity.

Social psychologists have determined that 98 percent of babies are creative, but by age sixteen only 3 percent of individuals display a similar measure of creativity. Many of those same clever and creative infants, now teenagers, spend much of their time looking at television or videos. They have images and sounds already packaged and ready for them at the flip of the button. This lifestyle requires them to use little imagination.

Reading could change that, as it activates all sorts of neurological pathways in the brain. When you read, your mind is at work on a larger scale because you are consciously, constantly laying down tracks on neurological pathways. Your mind recognizes and assembles letters, words, phrases, and sentences into meaning and converts that meaning into images that are stored away in your mind. The more often you do that, the better your imagination is nourished and stretched.

And that's all part of learning to think big and think better.

CHAPTER 20

In-Depth Learning

I n 1992, Audrey Jones accompanied her fifth-grade daughter on a class field trip to hear me give a presentation for elementary school kids at Johns Hopkins. We didn't meet that day, but Audrey and her daughter sat in the front row of Turner Auditorium, just a few feet from me as I told that audience about being the dummy in my fifth-grade class, how I'd come to be a brain surgeon, and what amazing potential there was in a normal human brain. I'm sure I also summarized the THINK BIG philosophy before challenging my young audience to use the amazing brain God had given them and think big about what they could do with their lives.

Four years later, a friend of Audrey's who worked at Johns Hopkins told her I was hiring a medical secretary. At least in part due to the favorable impression I made when she heard me speak, she decided to apply. Looking over her application and reading her qualifications (previous work for the American Visionary Art Museum during its founding and establishment, a college degree in psychology, and excellent references), I thought she was overqualified for the position. But we gladly hired her anyway.

She dug right in to learn my expectations along with her responsibilities — and soon displayed understanding and mastery of her position. At the same time, Audrey observed, asked questions, and learned what the other people around the office were doing. Some of her coworkers considered her nosey. But I attributed that to the fact too few people have the curiosity — or perhaps the determination and initiative — to do more than surface learning.

Audrey soon realized how the various jobs in our department fit together: which people interacted with each other, how, why, and when. She discovered ways to create efficiency and synergy in the way we worked together.

Six months after we'd hired Audrey, my administrative assistant became ill and had to give up her job. That sudden development could have thrown the entire pediatric neurosurgery department into a tailspin. But by that time, my new medical secretary not only understood the administrative assistant responsibilities, but she also had a good grasp on everyone else's in our large, very busy, specialized surgical practice. From initial patient screening, clinic appointments, radiology and surgery processing and scheduling, insurance and billings, the department budget, staffing issues, and more, Audrey stepped up, took charge without skipping a beat, and shortly ramped up the efficiency of the overall operation. Audrey says she knew once she got her foot in the door she would have the opportunity to advance.

She consistently demonstrated such good judgment that I soon trusted her to screen my calls and prioritize demands on my time. I wasn't the only one amazed by how she juggled so many diverse tasks every day and never seemed to let any of the balls drop. From parents calling in tears, pleading for us to take their child's case, to pushy media folks who never understood why I couldn't step out of surgery to give them a quick quote, or better yet "just a short interview" in time to get their story on the evening news, Audrey calmly and kindly handled all callers and inquiries.

For the last seventeen years of my career at Johns Hopkins, Audrey (as office manager) oversaw the daily operations of Johns Hopkins' Department of Pediatric Neurosurgery and functioned as surgical coordinator in charge of handling records and case files for several hundred surgical patients a year, my

OR calendar, and more. On top of all that she helped me juggle weekly speaking engagements, board meetings, media interviews, and correspondence. Somehow she kept my professional and personal schedules synchronized.

In short, she made herself invaluable—so much so that when I retired from my surgery post at Johns Hopkins, I hired her full time as my personal executive manager. (I hope and pray I can keep her on board for the rest of my life.)

Audrey's story illustrates, as well as any I know, this next-to-the-last letter in THINK BIG: "I" for In-depth learning. It could also stand for initiative, an essential factor of in-depth learning.

Learning at a deep level is for the sake of knowing and understanding much more than the simple facts of a subject. Asking and answering not only the obvious *what* question, but the *who*, *why*, *when*, and *how* questions as well—as opposed to people who cram, cram, cram to memorize what they hope are the "right" names, numbers, dates, lists, and rules they expect to see on a test. They may regurgitate facts on the exam, but three weeks later, they don't remember, let alone understand, any practical implications of that subject matter.

The more in-depth knowledge you acquire in any one area of interest makes you that much more of an expert—and that much more valuable among those in that field. But in-depth learning requires initiative. Audrey demonstrated that by also trying to understand everything she could about the other jobs in our office.

I could not have gotten a good, in-depth education in my poor inner-city high school if I had not taken the initiative to seek out my teachers after school. Further initiative took me to the Wayne State University library and campus, where I could have just looked at that advertisement for a lab assistant, shrugged my shoulders and thought, *I'm just a high school student. That's not for me.* Instead, I took the initiative to apply and get the position, which provided me a wealth of in-depth learning.

My high school education was enhanced and complemented by the in-depth knowledge acquired through my involvement in science fair competitions, forensic club events, field trips, visits to local museums, and ROTC responsibilities. The more experiences you get exposed to, the broader your horizons become and the greater the potential for deeper knowledge in a variety of areas.

My mother preached initiative as consistently as her life demonstrated it. Whenever my brother and I complained—about this person or that person, some situation or problem we faced, or any injustice we felt we'd suffered—she would often resurrect one of her favorite talking points. "The person who has the most to do with what happens to you and what you will do with your life is you!" she insisted. In other words, we needed to quit complaining, take some personal responsibility, and do something.

Curtis was gifted at math in high school. But he never did like geometry. He grumbled about the homework, proclaimed the problems "too hard" and "not really math," and rhetorically asked, "When will I ever use this stuff?"

Mother, of course, encouraged him to know it better than anyone in the class. So Curtis (a typical firstborn, compliant and eager to please) buckled down and learned geometry well enough to earn an A. Some years later, Curtis became an engineer who designed aircraft brakes, using geometric formulas and analytical skills on a regular basis.

Even if you've already decided on a career that does not relate to a subject you are currently studying, you may be surprised how, when, and where in-depth learning might be valuable. And since experts predict that a person entering today's workforce will change careers three to five times before retirement, in-depth learning will not only make you more valuable, but it may also give you more options in an era of growing specialization.

In order to effectively learn deeply, you must first decide how you learn best and recognize your preferred learning style. Some learn best using our auditory (listening) skills, taking in information through their ears rather than their eyes. Others learn by discussion, talking over a topic with others, perhaps in a study group, where dialogue raises questions and helps us see other people's points of view. Some people retain information better by repetition and drill, using learning tools like lists and flashcards. Still others acquire knowledge by doing an activity—hands-on or kinesthetic learning. Those like me learn best by reading. Most of us combine two or more styles to gain in-depth understanding.

To discover your strongest learning method, think of something you have enjoyed learning a lot about. Then ask yourself these questions: How did I learn that? What method or methods did I use? Then concentrate on using that style more consistently so you are working from your strengths.

Regardless of which method best suits you, in-depth learning requires serious, repetitive study. But useful knowledge—meaning retrievable when you need it—needs to be accessed on a regular basis. Your incredible brain processes and retains a constant deluge of information coming in from various senses. Everything you've ever seen, heard, done, read, or learned is still in there. But it's of no use unless you can retrieve it.

People get frustrated and say, "I read that a month ago. Why can't I remember it?" The more you access that information, the more solidly the neural pathways are laid down. The learning process is like walking across an open, grassy field. The first time you walk through the field, you leave little trace of your presence there, and you would be hard-pressed to walk back following the exact same path. However, the more you go back and forth across that field, the more you wear a path that you can confidently tread anytime you return. This is where the development of talent and in-depth learning overlap.

In his book, *This Is Your Brain on Music: The Science of a Human Obsession*, rocker-turned-neuroscientist Daniel J. Levitin reports, "In study after study of composers, basketball players, fiction writers, ice skaters, concert pianists, chess players, master criminals, and what have you, this number [10,000 hours] comes up again and again ... No one has yet found a case in which true world-class expertise was accomplished in less time."[9]

He goes on to say, "Learning requires the assimilation and consolidation of information in neural tissue. The more experiences we have with something, the stronger the memory/learning trace for that experience becomes."[10]

That's just another way of saying the more times you access your skill at woodcarving, your multiplication tables, a chemical formula, a piece of music, the proper steps required to change the oil in your car, or the muscle-memory needed to dribble a basketball between your legs and make a behind-the-back bounce-pass to a driving teammate, the wider and smoother the necessary neural pathways become. And the more varied methods and directions from which you access that knowledge, the easier the results of your in-depth learning come back to you, becoming almost instinctive or like a subconscious reflex.

■ ■ ■

Our educational system today rarely requires enough in-depth learning. Even students graduating near the top

---

9.   Daniel J. Levitin. *This Is Your Brain on Music*. (New York: Dutton, 2006).

10.   Ibid.

of their high school classes often don't understand how to dig beneath the surface to acquire deeper knowledge.

A few suggestions from my own experience:

1. Don't settle for "knowing" surface information and facts.
2. Don't just read the material once and hope to remember the general idea.

In med school, I would get up at six o'clock in the morning and read until eleven p.m. six days a week. Then I would quiz myself: "What did I just read? What were the key points in that chapter?" If I couldn't answer those questions, I'd go back and read it again. Each time I went back, I reinforced that pathway. It's no different than learning how to play the piano. You're not going to master it in one lesson. Repetition is key.

Instead of thinking small and focusing on specifics, think bigger and see the whole picture. Then you'll know and understand the specifics in the process. In med school, we often were given access to the previous year's exams as study aids. I quickly learned that I shouldn't memorize specific answers, because those weren't going to be on our tests. I learned, instead, to ask, "What body of information do I need to know in order to answer questions on this topic?" Or, "What is the subject matter these questions are getting at?" Then I'd dig deeper to understand the broader subjects and where the facts fit into the puzzle.

As you study, keep asking: What was I supposed to learn from this book? Why is it important for me to learn the material in this course? How and where might that knowledge be applied? What beneficial lesson can I take away from this experience? When you begin to think in broader and deeper terms like that, you've already separated yourself from the masses that tend to focus on little things.

No one needs to put in ten thousand hours for a subject or read from morning until night to benefit from in-depth learning.

In-depth knowledge accumulates from the time you start prob-
ing beneath the surface of any subject.

I recently heard the stories of two teenagers who didn't have
to wait long for their rewards. The first is Liron Bar, from the
town of Beersheba in southern Israel, who was only thirteen
years old when he created a phone app enabling users to track
incoming Palestinian rocket fire. A professional developer volunteered to help him produce and distribute the free app which,
upon recommendations from the Israeli military, is now used
to provide hundreds of thousands of people in southern Israel
an early alert and extra time to seek shelter and safety.[11] I don't
think Liron had reached the ten thousand-hour point when his
in-depth learning made him valuable to the people in southern
Israel.

And then seventeen-year-old Nick D'Aloisio from London,
England, sold an app he'd created to Yahoo. They paid him
thirty million dollars for the technology he designed, which uses
an algorithm to automatically create short, quick summaries of
news stories for mobile phones. Yahoo then gave him an office
at their London headquarters, where he planned to work while
finishing high school.[12]

Both boys proved that in-depth learning does indeed make
them more valuable to the people around them.

■ ■ ■

Once I discovered the difference in-depth learning could
make in my life, the change in my self-image alone was

11.   Stuart Winer. "New App Offers 'Sderot Experience.'" *The Times of
Israel.* Nov. 12, 2012, http://www.timesofisrael.com/new-app-offers-sderot-
experience-for-iphone-users.

12.   Brian Stelter. "Nick D'Aloisio, 17, Sells Summly App to Yahoo." *New
York Times.* Mar. 25, 2013. http://www.nytimes.com/2013/03/26/business/
media/nick-daloisio-17-sells-summly-app-to-yahoo.html?_r=0.

enough to make me want more. Then I found that goals and in-depth learning seemed to feed off each other. My goal of becoming a doctor gave me a sense of focus that made science interesting. I wanted to absorb everything I could, because it felt so on-target and useful. So the in-depth learning in my science classes seemed to take less effort and less discipline. That often happens naturally the higher you ascend the educational ladder. By the time they settle on a college major, most students find in-depth learning so relevant to their goals that the work doesn't feel as hard.

Graduate school, with its even-higher demands, consists mostly of in-depth learning. A lot of students find the most challenging graduate work to be their most satisfying educational experience.

Even if you haven't settled on any life goals, use the time you have to your advantage. Ask yourself, "What do I want to be doing six months from now? What do I want to have learned or accomplished a year from now? Two years from now? Five years from now?"

Set goals for yourself by concentrating on what you are good (or best) at. Most people enjoy what they are good at and are good at what they enjoy. Sometimes the knowledge that comes out of in-depth learning will focus and direct you toward your ultimate life goals.

One caution: Don't be so set on your goals that you run your race, eyes always straight ahead like a horse with blinders on, unable to see any other direction. Be wide-eyed and flexible enough to see where your learning might take you.

I once knew a young doctor in training who dreamed of becoming a neurosurgeon. He didn't do that well in his first residency so he transferred to another program with a different but also demanding surgical specialty. He struggled there, too, and became discouraged. However, in the course of his training he'd gotten fascinated by, and quite knowledgeable about, specialized computer technology in a new arena of medical learning and exploration. Someone recommended his expertise in this fledgling field of medicine at the same time I had been asked to consult on a case to separate another set of craniopagus Siamese twins in Singapore. This young doctor was such a help to me on that case and so impressed me with his expertise that I encouraged him to rethink his goals and turn in that direction for additional training.

Don't make the mistake of devaluing the in-depth knowledge you acquire along the way—it may lead you to think big in a new direction.

■ ■ ■

In the currency of information, the world is getting richer by the second ... make that nanosecond. It's estimated that human knowledge doubled once every century or so until 1900. By the middle of the twentieth century, it was doubling every twenty-five years. As I write this in 2014, overall human knowledge is doubling in a little over twelve months, and experts say the continued expansion will soon see a doubling of knowledge every twelve hours.[13]

What is perhaps even more mind-boggling about today's world is just how much of that information is literally at our fingertips, instantly available to us 24/7 in our smart phones, GoogleGlasses, iWatches, and the devices released since I wrote this sentence.

The problem with that is this: when our brain is exposed

---

13.   David Russell Schilling. "Knowledge Doubling Every 12 Months, Soon to Be Every 12 Hours." Industry Tap. Apr. 13, 2013. http://www. industrytap.com/knowledge-doubling-every-12-months-soon-to-be-every-12-hours/3950.

to new information, we process that new data based on what we already know. It's our in-depth knowledge, with the well-worn trails and many pathways, that enables us connect, analyze, integrate, understand, and then use that information in a productive way.

Be careful not to confuse information and knowledge. Information is mostly surface knowledge. The real power results from in-depth learning—accessing, understanding, and using the unfathomable knowledge our incredible human brains can contain.

CHAPTER 21

God

When I was a child, I imagined God as an old, old man with a long, white beard who lived in the clouds with a powerful telescope that could see through walls. He was always peering down to see what you did wrong and making sure you got punished for it. My early image of him was that he was distant, uncaring, and harsh, investing most of his time and energy ensuring no riffraff got into heaven. I clung to some of that concept as I grew up. This is why I found myself in early adulthood being extremely conservative about everything—to the point of being puritanical. I was judgmental of others' actions and attitudes, and I didn't always enjoy life.

I have slowly matured and have experienced God's help in many crises. I have come to realize that God does not want to punish us; rather, he wants to fulfill our lives. God created us, loves us, and wants to help us to realize our potential so that we can be useful to others.

Growing up without a man in our home forced me to look elsewhere for male role models. I didn't have a dad to turn to for help or advice when I got into trouble or wrestled with a decision I didn't know how to make. Thus, the heroes of the Bible became my heroes, as well as my role models. I learned about Jesus Christ, who gave himself for other people and cared about their pain. I admired Daniel and the three Hebrew boys (Shadrach, Meshach, and Abednego) who believed in God and stayed true to their principles—even when the king tried to put them to death.

The hero I related to most was Joseph in the Old Testament. Maybe I identified with him because he had to face the world without his family. I used to mull over his being alone and in prison in Egypt because his jealous brothers had sold him into slavery.

Somewhere during my childhood, I sincerely believed that God was capable of taking any person from any circumstance and doing something with that life. Joseph started in slavery but eventually became governor of Egypt. Not a bad role model, was he?

I now see God as a friend who wants what is best for me and for all of us. I have drawn that conclusion from seeing how he works in the lives of others. But mostly through experiencing his presence and influence in my own life:

- God played a role in my life the night that my mother prayed to him and asked for wisdom for her two sons.

- God was with me that day I gave my heart to him and decided I wanted to be a missionary doctor.

- He changed my life forever that afternoon in the bathroom as I read his Word in utter despair over almost killing my friend because of my uncontrollable temper.

And that was just the start of it. The list goes on right up to this day. I could not have written a script for my life and made it come out the way it did. I know my life's plan came from God. From my impoverished childhood, to my successes in school, to my years at Yale and in med school, throughout an unbelievable medical career, and all that has happened after my retirement from surgery, I could never have orchestrated all that. Only God could.

. . .

God—the "G" in THINK BIG—has been the greatest single influence in my life. Even though "G" is the last letter, it is certainly not the least important.

I want to share two stories that represent two situations, decades apart, when my faith in God influenced my responses.

First, about halfway through my time at Yale, I looked to the future and realized I had another ten years or so of training to go. With what I'd already heard about the demanding schedule I could expect in medical school, internship, and residency, I began to wonder, *When will I ever have time to develop a serious relationship?*

So I prayed, "Lord, bring the right person into my life before I get started on that track." And he did—right after that request, I met Candy. When I look back over the years, in terms of compatibility and the kind of person I needed, I could never have found a better choice.

I needed a wife who was independent and would have pursuits of her own. Someone secure enough in her own identity that she would not depend on the attentions of a spouse for self-worth or fulfillment. Someone comfortable with herself, so she could be confident of my love and support when I couldn't be with her to show it. And of course I wanted someone who was not only attractive, but also charming, talented, and smart.

Candy met all those criteria and more; she complements me. I'm a meticulous planner; she's spontaneous and fun. She is an extrovert to my introvert. She loves people, parties, and entertaining. My default is a quiet spot in some corner with something to read. The primary reason we have established so many wonderful friendships over the years is Candy—because she lives with her arms wide open accepting, welcoming, and loving others.

Candy and I both believe God brought us together for a purpose and blessed our relationship from the start. I thought she was the right person when I asked her to marry me. After thirty-nine years of marriage, I know she was—and is.

Second, in 2002, following some routine medical tests, I learned I had an aggressive form of prostate cancer. I had an MRI done to see if the cancer had metastasized, meaning spread to other parts of my body. After the MRI, the technician handed me an envelope with copies of the scans.

I carried the sheets of film back to my office and stuck the first one up on the light board. I am not a radiologist, but I'd seen enough scans over the years to know the series of spots up and down the spine did not look good. I took a moment to double-check the name on the border of the film. "Patient: Carson, Ben."

I am going to die from this, I thought. *I will be leaving Candy, our sons, my mother, and my brother to go on without me. All my plans for the future? I won't live long enough to do any of that.*

Word got out. I received hundreds of cards and letters from families of former patients, from people who had read my books, even a letter from the president and First Lady of the United States—all saying they were praying for me. (One woman called my office to say, "I heard Dr. Carson is dead! I want to speak to him.")

Six days later, I learned those spots on the MRI were abnormalities in my bone marrow, a condition I had been born with. Not cancer. But I still had cancer in my prostate. So I had prostate surgery, which successfully removed the cancer. And my doctor predicted a long, full life.

As a surgeon who literally held the life or death of my patients in my hands every day; my role was to choose life and prevent (or at least postpone) death. Death became a familiar enemy; and we worked hard to avoid it as much as possible. Although it rarely occurred, we were always cognizant of the potential in the operating room. And as a Christian I believed death marked not merely an end to be feared, but simply the end of one phase of life ... not the end of existence. I had never faced death myself until then.

I actually felt extremely grateful I had lived as long as I did. Facing my own mortality, I realized that because of my faith, death was not all that frightening. But the experience also prompted another realization: I couldn't imagine what it would be like to face death without a belief in God.

. . .

Gradually over the years, by regularly reading, studying, and depending on the advice in God's Word, I gained a more accurate picture of God. As a doctor and a scientist, the more I learn about creation and especially the human brain, the more impressed I am with how incredibly smart our Creator must be. I look through my operating microscope and marvel at the intricate complexities of creation inside a baby's brain. Or I stand under the stars on a summer night, looking up at a universe made with such precision that you can set clocks by it.

I see evidence everywhere of a brilliant and logical God who is unbelievably loving. What else could possibly explain why the all powerful Creator of the universe humbled himself and came to earth to be spat upon, cursed, even beaten with a whip, before he was crucified and died on a cross for the very same people who did that to him? A God that loving, instead of being quick to judge and anxious to condemn us for every little sin, is really an almost unimaginably forgiving God.

I finally realize that God's first concern is not about whether we abide by his rules or deserve his grace and forgiveness. His priority is right relationships. This personal relationship is all God has wanted from us since the beginning of time. It is what we were created for.

My relationship with God is like any other relationship in my life. How do I develop and maintain a personal relationship with any friend? We spend time together. I include him in my life. We talk. In the process, I know him better and the relationship grows stronger. And the more time we spend together, the closer we become.

Some friends become so close because of the experiences they've gone through together, they might not even need to speak to communicate with one another. A glance or an expression or a laugh conveys much between them. My relationship with God is a lot like that. First thing every morning when Candy and I pray and read the Bible, we spend time together with Him. We tell God the plans and concerns we have, and ask Him to be with us throughout the day. At night we thank him for His presence, ask His forgiveness for any mistakes we've made, and read more from Proverbs.

When God inspired my parents to give me the middle name of Solomon, he must have known I would have a lifelong love for the book of Proverbs, which King Solomon wrote. I see the irony in the fact that Solomon, early in his reign, made his reputation for great wisdom when he settled a dispute between two women arguing over who was the rightful mother of a child by proposing they divide the baby in half. In my early career I too made a name for myself professionally by dividing babies—when we separated the Binder twins. So I feel an affinity for Solomon. I only wish I could be half as wise.

During the course of the day, I ask God to give me wisdom to use my talents well and to use the knowledge I have to provide me perspective, insight, understanding, and truth, particularly when difficult situations arise. I ask him to give me the right words in hard or unpleasant conversations. I have prayed before and during every surgery.

God not only gives me those things, but also a confidence that what I am doing is right. That confidence is contagious.

I need that kind of self-confidence to deal with the publicity that I have received at such an early age in a field like neurosurgery. It does not matter what you are doing in a field like this, if you achieve fame, some people invariably come along and accuse you of stealing their patients, of being hungry for publicity, or even of being a charlatan. At some time in our lives all of us have felt the sting of undeserved criticism—the point at which we can then say, "God, I am doing my best. Give me peace." And God is always there with us.

You may wonder if my talking to God is a real, two-way conversation—if he talks back to me. Every time I read the Bible, I ask God to speak to me through it. And that regularly happens. I can't count the number of times, starting that afternoon I stabbed my friend, when I have read a verse that spoke directly to a situation I was facing or would face later in the day.

I recently heard the word *conversation* defined as communication intended to guide or direct each other's thoughts. By this definition I have a lot of conversations with God. Most often he guides my thoughts through Scripture or speaks to me through others: a friend who calls with timely advice; a rejuvenating hug from a young patient on an exhausting day; or an encouraging smile from a colleague who just happens to walk by right when I need patience to deal with the person I'm talking to at the time.

Sometimes the messages are just reminders that God is there with me. But many times he gives a new thought, an insight, or an idea that I know I didn't conjure up on my own. The Creator of the universe, who has demonstrated his love for me, who made me in his image, who designed my incredible brain, actually knows my mind and guides my thoughts.

God is central to my THINK BIG philosophy. He is the source of all the **Talents** within us—and the revealer of talents, if we ask him. He defines not just **Honesty**, but also right and wrong. God offers us **Insight**, wisdom, and truth, but he has also given us brains with huge frontal lobes so we can process, analyze, understand, and apply it.

God's Golden Rule pretty well sums up what it means to be **Nice**, and Jesus had much to say about how we should treat others. God, the omniscient one, is the ultimate source of all **Knowledge**. And he's glad to help when we turn to him for the wisdom to use it. He is also the author of the bestselling **Book** of all time. More people have read the Bible and relied on it than any other book in history. Its timeless truths have never become outdated or irrelevant. Who else but an infinite God could help us discover and use **In-Depth Learning**?

God has given us everything we need to think big. He is what ties it all together. So the better we know the One who designed our brains, the bigger and better we'll be able to think. Because we cannot ever think bigger than God.

CHAPTER 22

Think Big

Since railroad tracks ran right along the route Curtis and I walked to Wilson Junior High School, the fastest and most exciting way to get to school was to hop one of the freight trains rolling on the tracks in the direction we were going. We jogged alongside the train, jumped, caught the railing, held on until we got our footing, and then climbed up and onto the train. Sometimes we also had to dodge the railroad security men who would have stopped us if they'd spotted us.

Curtis was two years older, bigger, faster, and stronger. He liked the challenge of faster-moving trains, tossing his clarinet case onto one flatcar and then jumping to catch ahold on the last car of the train. He knew if he missed his chance, he risked never seeing his band instrument again. But that never happened.

Being younger and smaller, I preferred the slower-moving trains.

In retrospect, I realize it was quite dangerous either way. Then a boy we knew slipped while trying to jump a train, fell onto the tracks, and lost a leg. My brain started working then, and I considered the danger for the first time. I thought, *That guy was certainly more athletic than I am.* And my relatively quick conclusion was that if he could get hurt that way, I could too.

Yet even hearing that story about a boy maimed for life didn't bring an end to our risky choice of transportation. We stopped only after an encounter I had with a different threat as I trotted along the empty tracks on my way to school alone one morning. Near one of the railroad tracks, a gang of bigger boys, all of them white, approached me. One kid, carrying a big stick, yelled, "Hey, you! Nigger boy!"

I froze and stared at the ground. He whacked me across the shoulders with the stick as his buddies crowded around. They called me dirty names and told me "nigger kids" didn't belong at Wilson Junior High. I was too small to fight them and too scared to run.

When they yelled, "Get out of here as fast as you can run. If we ever catch you around here again, we'll kill you!" I took off running and didn't slow down until I reached the schoolyard.

I told Curtis what had happened, and from then on we took a different route to school. I never hopped another train and never saw that gang again.

I tell that story because how we understand and deal with risk can interfere with our ability to think big in two basic ways. Our fear of failure, embarrassment, or the unknown could keep us from taking appropriate risks required to set and reach goals or achieve success. So some people never take the risk and never begin to use their potential.

Other people never give serious thought to the pitfalls in any of their decisions and end up taking huge and senseless risks — perhaps ruining their lives and the lives of the people around them. Thinking big requires learning to identify, choose, and live with acceptable risk.

Let me tell you how I learned to do that.

Not long after my first hemispherectomy with Maranda Francisco, a family who'd read about her case brought their thirteen-year-old daughter from New Mexico to see me. She'd been having constant intractable seizures for two months that had already taken a terrible toll on her body. Unable to control her breathing, she'd undergone a tracheostomy, so she couldn't talk. She also had pulmonary problems that presented surgical risks all by themselves. Her medical condition was terrible and deteriorating by the day.

The focus points of her seizures were in troublesome areas of the brain, making this surgery more dangerous than the previous hemispherectomies we'd done. On top of that we worried that her brain wouldn't have the elasticity of the younger children in previous cases. So we didn't know how much permanent function this young teenager might lose if she did survive.

My colleagues and I felt that this young lady would be a good candidate for the radical surgery. However, there was a famous neurologist at Johns Hopkins who thought operating would be foolish and that the patient was certainly going to die. He went so far as to write letters to the department head, the president, and the CEO of the hospital to stop this. But when this neurologist had to travel to a conference and was no longer on the hospital site, my colleagues and I decided to go ahead.

I explained to this girl's parents, as I did to any parents of children needing this radical procedure, "If we don't do anything, your daughter is going to die. If we attempt this procedure, she still may die. But at least she has a chance."

The operation went surprisingly well. She remained in a coma for several days, but when she awakened, she had stopped seizing. By the time she went home, she was talking again. When that neurologist returned from his conference, she was doing extremely well. Weeks later she went back to school and continued making steady improvement.

In the aftermath of that case, I thought a lot about the risk I had been willing to take. As a neurosurgeon, I lived with a certain amount of risk every day. But the risk had been much greater in this controversial case. How had I come to the position I took? What made me so sure it was the right decision! When was any risk worth taking? How and when would I consider a surgical risk too great to take?

I recall rolling the questions around in my mind, looking back at my decision process from every angle. And it was during the process of deciding whether to do the surgery or not when I came up with the four questions for what I call my Best/Worst Analysis (B/WA) formula.

- What is the best thing that can happen if I do this?
- What is the worst thing that can happen if I do this?
- What is the best thing that can happen if I don't do it?
- What is the worst thing that can happen if I don't do it?

I've used the B/WA a thousand times since, whenever I've faced hard decisions. This simple risk-analysis approach can be applied to almost any troublesome decision we face individually, corporately in a group, even on a national level.

Try it on any decisions you're grappling with right now. In most cases, by the time you've answered all four questions, your decision will be much easier because you'll have identified the most acceptable risk and you'll be able to proceed with confidence rather than feeling paralyzed by uncertainty and fear.

· · ·

I'm not only encouraging individuals to use the brain God gave them to take responsibility for themselves and think big to pursue the success they are capable of. Now I'm trying to inspire Americans (of all sizes, colors, and political parties) to use the incredible brainpower we've each been given, pool our resources, and think big together about reasonable ways we can tackle and solve the issues and challenges our country faces today.

The subject matter in many of my speeches has been a little different lately as I've promoted the message of my two latest books—*America the Beautiful: Rediscovering What Made This Nation Great* and *One Nation: What We Can All Do to Save America's Future*. The challenge I'm giving to audiences today has a clear connection to what I've been saying for years.

In fact, every element of the THINK BIG philosophy can apply as easily to us as a nation, as they do to us individually.

T—There has never been a nation in the history of the world with the combined talents, strengths, and resources that America has today.

H—Let's restore and maintain our nation's integrity, trustworthiness, and honesty, and revisit the values upon which this country was founded.

I—Insight and the reasoning power of our brains can enable us to apply wisdom and truth to our nation's problems.

N—If we are nice, take ourselves out of the middle, and listen to one another, we can establish respectful dialogue with those of differing views and find common ground from which, and on which, to rebuild our foundation of unity.

K—Let's use our twenty-first-century knowledge wisely to find common-sense solutions to immigration, energy, unemployment, and a host of such issues.

B—If we avail ourselves of books, magazines, news, the Internet, and other resources, we can better understand and participate in America's public life.

I—We need to take initiative and responsibility to do some in-depth learning—not just about celebrity pop culture, but about current national and world issues and America's foundational principles and history.

G—We live in a country today where people are always saying, "You can't talk about God in public!" But if a belief in God was important enough to be cited in our nation's Declaration of Independence, if "under God" is in our Pledge of Allegiance, if the walls of courtrooms across our land as well as every coin in our pockets and every bill in our wallets say "In God We Trust," perhaps we ought to allow our lives to speak at least as loudly as our money. It's all right to live by godly principles: loving our fellow man, caring for our neighbors, and living in service by developing and using our God-given talents and resources to be of greater value to the people and the nations around us.

As President Ronald Reagan said in his first inaugural address, "We [American people] are too great a nation to limit ourselves to small dreams."[14] And we are too great to think small.

So many people around the country have embraced and agreed with that message wherever I've spoken that a growing number of folks have encouraged me to throw my hat in the political ring, and run for president of the United States. The size and response of the crowds—some of whom greet me with chants of "Run, Ben, run!"—have forced me to give the possibility more serious consideration than I ever thought I would.

I began to consider, write, and speak about my concerns for America and my thoughts on common-sense ways to address those issues quite some time before I made the decision to retire. And because of my passion for my country, I expect to keep speaking out about the most critical issues facing our nation—whatever I decide about any political venture.

Fortunately, as I'm wrapping up this book, the time to make a decision has not yet arrived. But it soon will. When it does, I know I'll need to think bigger than I ever have before. And I'll have to use all the lessons I've shared here to make the decision—whichever way it goes.

No matter what the future holds, Candy and I dream of, and hope we live to see, a nationwide network of at least one hundred thousand Carson Scholars all over America maturing into young adults who continue to develop and use their intellectual prowess, while also demonstrating compassion and care for others. What a powerful leadership base that could provide for our nation!

---

14. "Inaugural Address," January 20, 1981, Ronald Reagan Presidential Library and Museum, http://www.reagan.utexas.edu/archives/speeches/1981/12081a.htm.

That's a dream we intend to keep pursuing. And we fully expect that dream to come true.

One reason I believe, more than ever, that dreams can come true—sometimes in unexpected ways—is because of so many supporting experiences throughout my life. One recent occasion served as a wonderful reminder.

In the spring of 2012, Candy and I traveled to Africa as honorees at the inauguration of the Benjamin S. Carson School of Medicine at Babcock University, a couple hours' drive from Lagos, Nigeria. Sitting on the platform, waiting to give my address, I looked out over the graduates and the crowd of fifty thousand people who came to the university's commencement. And I remembered my childhood dream of becoming a missionary doctor. That was my life goal for a number of years, until I realized God had other ideas for me. Because I followed God's plan, rather than my own, I've been able to share my faith and God's love for the world in more ways, and to have greater influence on more people than I probably could have as a missionary.

And now I was in Africa, opening a Christian medical school that would train many doctors, who will in turn develop their own ministry of healing throughout Africa and hopefully around the world. This just goes to show that God's plans for us are always better than the plans we have for ourselves. If we read and obey his Word and follow Jesus, he may just surprise us and enable us to do greater things than we might have imagined on our own. Isaiah 55:9 reminds us of this by saying his thoughts and ways are higher than ours. In other words, he designed and desires us to dream and think big, but he can always think, and do, bigger.

God has given you a resource of unimaginable power and infinite potential to pursue unlimited opportunities. What you do with it is your choice.

You have a brain. Use it to think big.

Personal Talent Assessment

1.   Settle down in a quiet spot where you won't be interrupted for a few minutes. Write or type your answers so you'll be able to go back later to add to them, study them, and think about them some more. List as many answers to each question as you can.

2.   Be honest, but also generous with yourself. To do well at something does not mean you have to do it perfectly.

  a.   What have I done well so far in life?

  b.   In what school subjects have I done well?

  c.   Why did I choose those subjects?

  d.   What are some reasons I did well in those classes?

  e.   What do I like to do that has caused others to compliment me?

  f.   What do I do well and think of as fun—that my friends see only as work or as a boring activity?

  g.   What are ten of my favorite things to do? Do I see a pattern or trend here? Circle similar things or draw lines to show where you see connections.

3.   Analyze yourself and your situation. Look back over your answers and consider any skills, characteristics, personality traits, interests, gifting, etc. referenced there, and begin a list of those talent factors you feel you have. Look for patterns, related traits, or complementary abilities.

4. Make a list of careers you've given previous thought to or could see yourself considering. Which of your talent factors could be useful in those careers?

5. Now look for matches again, but coming from the opposite direction. Start with several of your strongest character traits, skills, interests, and gifts—then try to imagine what sorts of careers would best use those strengths.

6. Do as much analysis on your own, depending on your personal observations and experience. When you've done all you can on your own, sit down with two or three other people, preferably one at a time, to go through the same list of questions. These should be individuals you respect and who know you well: a parent or family member, a coach or a teacher, a mentor, maybe one of your closest friends. Write down what they say they see as your strengths. Compare their feedback to the talent lists you've made on your own. What did they see in you that you hadn't seen for yourself?

7. When you've finished the exercise, spend a block of time (as much as an hour) every day for the next four to five days reexamining the answers.

8. Repeat the process every year or so. The beginning or end of a school year would be a logical time. Compare your analyses from year to year and note any differences you see: what interests are changing, what personality traits have become more obvious, what new skills or talents are developing.

DISCUSSION QUESTIONS FOR YOU HAVE A BRAIN

- Has anyone ever asked you, "Do you have a brain?" or something similar? If you were asked that question now, after you've finished reading this book, how would you respond?

- Is there someone in your life who believes in you even after you make a mistake? Why do you think that person is always there for you? How can you live up to their expectations?

- In chapter 2, Dr. Carson talks about trying out his new BB gun with his brother, Curtis. They were having fun until they realized the BBs that missed their target had damaged their neighbor's property. Think of a time you accidently broke something or upset someone because you didn't consider the full impact of your actions. What did you do? How did you make things right?

- God gave you your brain for a reason. What do you think your brain is for? What are you best at? What kind of career could you see yourself having in the future? And how will you get there?

- In chapter 3, Dr. Carson tells us about how one of his cousins, someone he looked up to, got involved with the wrong people and ended up losing his life. Do you know anyone who made bad decisions—whether it was drinking or doing drugs or stealing or hanging out with negative influences—and got hurt or in trouble because of it? If you could, how would you help that person to make better choices?

- Dr. Carson tells us of the day he decided to accept Jesus into his life. Do you have a relationship with God or do you believe in a supreme being? What is your relationship with that being like? Do you think becoming closer to him could help you grow as a person or achieve your goals?

- Have you ever had a teacher like Mr. Jaeck or Mrs. Miller, someone who helped you develop a strong interest in a subject and/or helped you grow your confidence? If you haven't, what would you want your mentor to be like? How would he or she help you?

- Dr. Carson read a lot of books when he was young—at least two a week, and that was on top of homework and chores! How many books do you read in a week or in a month? What kinds of books do you like to read most? Which books have stuck with you long after you finished the last page?

- Think of a time when you've gotten too upset over something trivial, like when Dr. Carson's mom bought him pants that weren't fashionable and would keep him from getting into the popular crowd. Why did you get mad? If you were in the same situation now, how would you react differently?

- Have you ever gotten answers or guidance in a dream, the way Dr. Carson did before his chemistry exam? Or perhaps you've dreamt about events that then happened shortly thereafter. What was that experience like? Where do you think those dreams came from?

- Have you ever set a goal—like Dr. Carson's goal to become a neurosurgeon—where the odds seemed stacked against you? Maybe someone said "you're not smart enough for that" or "only boys can play this sport" or "no one else has ever done this before." How did you react? Did you keep pursuing your goal? If you didn't, would you do things differently now?

- Is there someone in your life who is an overcomer? Someone like Sonya Carson, who faces obstacles but always finds a way to get past them and grow stronger? Maybe that person is a parent, a sibling, or a friend. What can you learn from them? How can you be an overcomer when it comes to your own challenges?

- Which of Dr. Carson's THINK BIG topics—Talent, Honesty, Insight, Nice, Knowledge, Books, In-Depth Learning, God— do you think would be easiest for you to live by? Which one would be the hardest? Why?

- After taking the Personal Talent Assessment at the back of the book, what are some careers you think would be a good fit for you? Which ones excite you most? Did any of the results surprise you?

- Now that you've read this book, how are you going to THINK BIG in your everyday life?

Gifted Hands, Revised Kids Edition

The Ben Carson Story

Gregg Lewis, Deborah Shaw Lewis

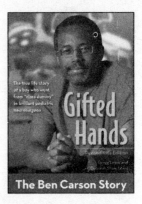

When Ben Carson was in school, his class-mates called him the class dummy. Many—including Ben himself—doubted that he would ever amount to anything. But his mother never let him quit. She encouraged Ben to do better and reach higher for his dreams, and eventually he discovered a deep love of learning. Today this young boy from the inner-city is one of the world's greatest pediatric neurosurgeons. Through determination and lot of hard work, Ben overcame his many obstacles and is now dedicated to saving the lives of critically ill children around the world.

Available in stores and online!

America the Beautiful

Rediscovering What Made This Nation Great

Ben Carson, M.D. with Candy Carson

What is America becoming? Or, more importantly, what can she be if we reclaim a vision for the things that made her great in the first place?

In America the Beautiful, Dr. Ben Carson helps us learn from our past in order to chart a better course for our future.

From his personal ascent from inner-city poverty to international medical and humanitarian acclaim, Carson shares experiential insights that help us understand
... what is good about America
... where we have gone astray
... which fundamental beliefs have guided America from her founding into preeminence among nations

Written by a man who has experienced America's best and worst firsthand, America the Beautiful is at once alarming, convicting, and inspiring. You'll gain new perspectives on our nation's origins, our Judeo-Christian heritage, our educational system, capitalism versus socialism, our moral fabric, healthcare, and much more.

An incisive manifesto of the values that shaped America's past and must shape her future, America the Beautiful calls us all to use our God-given talents to improve our lives, our communities, our nation, and our world.

Available in stores and online!

Think Big

Unleashing Your Potential for Excellence

Ben Carson, M.D., with Cecil Murphey

This book is for you if you have no dreams at all. It's for you if you've bought the lie that you'll never amount to anything. That's not true. Your life is BIG—far bigger than you've imagined.

Inside these pages lie the keys to recognizing the full potential of your life. You won't necessarily become a millionaire (though you might), but you will attain a life that is rewarding, significant, and more fruitful than you ever thought possible.

The author of this book knows about hardship. Ben Carson grew up in inner-city Detroit. His mother was illiterate. His father had left the family. His grade-school classmates considered Ben stupid. He struggled with a violent temper. In every respect, Ben's harsh circumstances seemed only to point to a harsher future and a bad end. But that's not what happened.

By applying the principles in this book, Ben rose from his tough life to one of amazing accomplishments and international renown. He learned that he had potential, he learned how to unleash it, and he did.

You can too. Put the principles in this book in motion. Things won't change overnight, but they will change. You can transform your life into one you'll love, bigger than you've ever dreamed.

Available in stores and online!

Gifted Hands

The Ben Carson Story

Ben Carson, M. D., with Cecil Murphey

Dr. Ben Carson is known around the world for breakthroughs in neurosurgery that have brought hope where no hope existed. In Gifted Hands, he tells of his inspiring odyssey from his childhood in inner-city Detroit to his position as director of pediatric neurosurgery at John Hopkins Medical Institutions at age thirty-three. Taking you into the operating room where he has saved countless lives, Ben Carson is a role model for anyone who attempts the seemingly impossible.

Filled with fascinating case histories, this bestselling book tells the dramatic and intimate story of Ben Carson's struggle to beat the odds—and of the faith and genius that make him one of today's greatest life-givers.

Available in stores and online!